# THE GOSPEL OF
# ISAIAH

# THE GOSPEL OF ISAIAH

By

Allan A. MacRae

MOODY PRESS
CHICAGO

*Printed in the United States of America*

# Contents

Contents

# Introduction

THIS IS NOT A FOREWORD but rather an introduction to a person, Dr. Allan A. MacRae.

Dr. MacRae was the recognized outstanding student of the renowned Dr. Robert Dick Wilson of old Princeton. Dr. Robert Dick Wilson was considered by many to be the greatest scholar of Semitic languages in the world in his day, and Dr. MacRae was, and is, a gifted follower of the same scholarship and tradition.

I had studied some classical and biblical Greek before entering seminary but knew nothing of Hebrew. Dr. MacRae was my teacher, and although Hebrew and the Semitic languages have not been the special field into which the Lord has taken me, I have always been glad for the base it provided for my studies.

Later Dr. MacRae was my professor in studying the Old Testament prophetical books and in this did much to sharpen my thinking in regard to the study of the original manuscripts and to exegesis in general—and in particular the exegesis of the eschatological passages throughout the Bible.

Toward the end of my seminary studies, he and I became close friends, and in my senior seminary year he employed me (I was already married to Edith, and Priscilla had just been born!) as a kind of assistant. Perhaps it would be better termed a helper in whatever odds and ends needed doing—from filing endless papers inside magazines (which was his filing system) to doing some of the rough-hewn research work on the exegesis of some Old Testament books, including Isaiah. I look back to those years as pleasant years as well as profitable ones for me.

## Introduction

Dr. MacRae has carried on the tradition of Robert Dick Wilson. His scholarship has helped countless young men and women to understand the weaknesses of liberal theology's view of the Bible. He has stood, and stands, for the Bible as without error in all areas: that is, in history and the things of interest to science as well as in religious matters. This, of course, bears directly on the consideration of the book of Isaiah. Dr. MacRae's deep knowledge of the cognate Semitic languages, as well as Hebrew, provides a base for a study in depth. This has never been more needed than in the present confusion in the Christian, and even evangelical, world.

I must say that because my present project (*How Should We Then Live?*) has almost completely taken up my last two and a half years, I have not been able to read the manuscript for the book nor the galleys for it; but that does not hinder me from writing a warm introduction to this scholar, Dr. Allan A. MacRae, who provides a bridge from the scriptural faithfulness of the great scholars of old Princeton Seminary, right up into the same discussions, in a slightly different form, which exist in our own day.

FRANCIS A. SCHAEFFER

# Preface

THE PURPOSE of this treatment of Isaiah 40:1—56:8 is to examine its great themes and to study their interrelations. It is hoped that the work will be useful to ministers and to other Bible students, whether they have knowledge of the original languages or not.

The book is not intended to be a commentary on this section of Isaiah. There are a number of good commentaries, written from various viewpoints, that contain helpful discussions of particular words and phrases. The main purpose of this writing is to open up the treasures of this section of the book by showing the interrelation of the thoughts and the general progress of the ideas presented.

Of course, such a treatment could not properly be written without careful examination and detailed study of each verse in the original Hebrew. Results of such study will be presented wherever it seems vital to the purpose of the discussion.

Since the book is not a commentary, one will not always find the author's interpretation of a passage immediately after its translation. In this section of Isaiah the passages are often closely related, and the material that precedes a portion of the translation may well be vital to its understanding.

Minor questions of detailed interpretation will be skipped. Discussions of points where the precise meaning of a word or phrase needs to be considered from a technical viewpoint will be included wherever: (1) the exact understanding of the original is vital to following the argument as a whole, or (2) the correct understanding of the passage requires an interpretation of the original that differs in an important respect from the rendering of the King James Version or of some widely used modern translation.

Discussions that require reference to the original wording will be given in such a way that they can be understood by those not familiar with the Hebrew language. Readers familiar with Hebrew will find the Hebrew word or form mentioned in "Notes to Particular Points."

Since all the classical Hebrew that has been preserved is contained in the Old Testament, any reader can test the validity of statements about the meaning of words by using Young's or Strong's concordance to find all the occurrences of a Hebrew word and then examining the context of each rendering.

Other writers will rarely be mentioned by name, since this is an attempt to study the various parts of this section of Isaiah in relation to one another and to gather and present evidence from the text itself, rather than to compare views of various interpreters. Where several writers take a view that seems unwarranted, reference is sometimes made in a general way and the contrary evidence presented. The author does not desire to speak with great positiveness except where the Scripture itself is positive and clear. If two views are equally possible, both are mentioned.

Throughout the book the word "section" will be used to point to the entire section of Isaiah that is the subject of the present discussion (40:1—56:8) and will be restricted to this use.

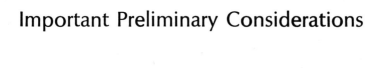

Important Preliminary Considerations

# 1

## Isaiah Sees the Saviour

AMONG THE OLD TESTAMENT prophetical books none is better known than Isaiah. Not only does it contain some of the grandest literature ever produced; it also contains some of the fullest and clearest statements of God's relation to suffering humanity.

To the Christian, no part of Isaiah is more important than the unified section that begins in chapter 40 and runs to the middle of chapter 56. This section contains more verses that are quoted in the New Testament than any other Old Testament passage of equal length. From it are drawn several of the most beautiful portions of Handel's *Messiah,* that oratorio so greatly loved by Christians. No chapter in the whole Old Testament presents the sufferings of Christ more vividly or sets forth their purpose more clearly than Isaiah 53. Every true Christian should love this great section of Isaiah.

Yet it must be said that for most Christians the section seems to consist of a long collection of isolated verses, most of which mean little to him. It contains many beautiful gems, but the passages between them often seem comparatively meaningless. It is as if one were walking through a dark tunnel, and only occasionally passing a small opening through which he might obtain a glimpse of a beautiful distant panorama, as the prophet looks forward to some thrilling aspect of the life of Christ.

This is particularly true of one of the unique features of this section—its depiction of "the Servant of the LORD." At point after point there are glimpses of this important figure, of whom it is said in Isaiah 53:11: "By his knowledge shall my righteous servant justify many." Several fairly long passages present aspects of this subject. Yet it is introduced almost casually, and the many references to it include a number that seem to contradict one another. Sometimes it seems to be a term for the entire nation of Israel. At other times it seems to designate a single individual. As one goes through the section, carefully examining these passages in relation to their context, the answer slowly emerges, and it is fascinating to see how the various strands are woven together.

The present writer has devoted many years to the study of this section of Isaiah and has concluded that it has a wonderful unity, even though this unity sometimes lies below the surface. There are certain rather unique principles of arrangement which, if securely grasped, make the whole section meaningful and thrilling. In this book he is attempting to present clearly the insights that the Lord has given him. It is his hope that each reader may be able to see the passage in a new light and to understand the interrelation of its parts, the real unity that runs through it all, and the gradual process of thought that reaches its great climax in its thrilling account of "the sufferings of Christ, and the glory that should follow" (1 Pet 1:11).

There is a sharp break between this section and the preceding chapters. At the end of the historical section that runs from Isaiah 36 through Isaiah 39, the prophet declared that the people of Judah would eventually be carried off into Babylonian captivity. Chapter 40 begins with a declaration of forgiveness of sin and a prediction of the coming of John the Baptist. In the familiar and beloved King James Version its first five verses read:

> (1) Comfort ye, comfort ye my people, saith your God. (2) Speak ye comfortably to Jerusalem, and cry unto her, that her warfare is accomplished, that her iniquity is pardoned: for she hath received of the LORD's hand double for all her sins. (3) The voice of him that crieth in the wilderness, Prepare ye the way of the LORD, make straight in the desert a highway for our God. ( 4) Every valley shall be exalted, and every mountain and hill shall be made low: and the crooked shall be made straight, and the rough places plain: (5) And the glory of the

LORD shall be revealed, and all flesh shall see it together: for the mouth of the LORD hath spoken it.

Following these wonderful verses we find other subjects of quite a different nature. At first their variety may seem bewildering. We shall now glance at a few of them. For instance, 41:5-7 reads:

> (5) The isles saw it, and feared; the ends of the earth were afraid, drew near, and came. (6) They helped every one his neighbor; and every one said to his brother, Be of good courage. (7) So the carpenter encouraged the goldsmith, and he that smootheth with the hammer him that smote the anvil, saying, It is ready for the sodering: and he fastened it with nails, that it should not be moved.

Chapter 42 sounds still different. Its first four verses read:

> (1) Behold my servant, whom I uphold; mine elect, in whom my soul delighteth; I have put my spirit upon him: he shall bring forth judgment to the Gentiles. (2) He shall not cry, nor lift up, nor cause his voice to be heard in the street. (3) A bruised reed shall he not break, and the smoking flax shall he not quench: he shall bring forth judgment unto truth. (4) He shall not fail nor be discouraged, till he have set judgment in the earth: and the isles shall wait for his law.

After these wonderful verses, which immediately bring the meek and gentle Saviour before our eyes, verses 13 to 15 of the same chapter sound almost like the war cry of one filled with despair:

> (13) The LORD shall go forth as a mighty man, he shall stir up jealousy like a man of war: he shall cry, yea, roar; he shall prevail against his enemies. (14) I have long time holden my peace; I have been still, and refrained myself: now will I cry like a travailing woman; I will destroy and devour at once. (15) I will make waste mountains and hills, and dry up all their herbs; and I will make the rivers islands, and I will dry up the pools.

Isaiah 46:11 describes God's purpose in very strange terms,

picturing Him as "calling a ravenous bird from the east, the man that executes my counsel from a far country: yea, I have spoken it, I will also bring it to pass; I have purposed it, I will also do it."

One wonders how to relate such a prediction as this to the coming of Christ. Yet Isaiah 49:1-2 brings us directly into His presence:

> (1) Listen, O isles, unto me; and hearken, ye people, from far; the LORD hath called me from the womb; from the bowels of my mother hath he made mention of my name. (2) And he hath made my mouth like a sharp sword; in the shadow of his hand hath he hid me, and made me a polished shaft; in his quiver hath he hid me.

The picture of Christ continues vividly for a number of verses leading up to the beautiful picture in verse 10. What a contrast is found in Isaiah 51:20!

> Thy sons have failed, they lie at the head of all the streets, as a wild bull in a net; they are full of the fury of the LORD, the rebuke of thy God.

Yet only two chapters later we reach the very familiar picture of the sacrifice of Christ in Isaiah 53.

Isaiah's wonderful predictions of Christ bring joy to every Christian heart. They are not, as they might seem at first sight, glorious passages intermixed with material that is quite unrelated. In the whole section, all the way from chapter 40 to chapter 56, there is a steady progress of thought, though it sometimes takes a bit of study to see how it develops. The section might be compared to a human body, in which many different portions are joined together by a skeleton that lies below the surface. In order to see this progress, certain important principles must be noted. Before we begin to examine the chapters in order, it will be helpful to look at some of these principles, noting relevant passages. So, in the next five chapters we shall give particular attention to the following:

1. The relation of Isaiah to his own times

2. God's provision for deliverance from exile; the king of Persia as deliverer
3. The reason for the sharp transitions that occur so frequently, particularly in chapters 40 through 48; the "symphonic structure"
4. The unusual treatment of sin; Isaiah's method of making clear the real cause of the Exile
5. The special importance of chapter 40 and its difference from the following chapters

Up to this point all quotations have been taken from the King James Version. In subsequent chapters, quotations from Isaiah 40:1—56:8 will always represent the author's own translation from the Hebrew, unless otherwise indicated, while quotations from other books of the Bible or other parts of Isaiah will use the King James Version.

# 2

# Isaiah and His Contemporaries

IT IS QUITE ERRONEOUS to think of the prophets as men sitting in ivory towers, dreaming of events in the distant future and writing books that would be of little value until centuries after they had been written.

The Old Testament makes it very clear that the prophets were vitally interested in the situations of their own time. Much of what they said consisted of rebuke for the sin of their contemporaries, and sometimes these sins were of a type rarely found today. The prophets were greatly interested in the attitudes of the contemporary rulers and would frequently point out God's desire for the handling of particular situations.

In some places these messages seem to have little relevance to our own time. Yet we can know that God caused them to be preserved as part of His holy Book because He intended that they should have a real meaning for us. Sometimes this meaning relates directly to our circumstances; in other cases careful study will reveal analogies that are useful in ascertaining God's will today.

The Old Testament prophets declared God's intention in particular situations and also gave remarkable predictions about the more distant future. It is easy to fasten our attention on one type of material to the exclusion of the other, but God desires His people to seek to understand every part of His Word. Those passages that may seem more interesting to us generally become more understandable when we connect them with the passages that were particularly related to their own immediate situation.

Even the messages that predict events that would not occur

until the distant future had a purpose in warning or reassuring the prophet's contemporaries. If we are to understand these future predictions correctly, we need also to study the messages that relate particularly to the prophet's own day.

The relation of Isaiah to his contemporaries is somewhat more complicated in this section of his book than in the usual situation. As in the case of all the prophets, he gave messages that would help the Israelites to whom he spoke and would also bring spiritual blessing to people in the distant future. In this particular case there was an additional purpose involved. Here the LORD led him so to write that a third group would receive special benefit—a group made up of people who would be living a century and a half after his time.

In the first thirty-five chapters of his book, Isaiah frequently pointed out the certainty that God's people would be taken into exile. At the end of chapter 39, just before our present section, he specifically declared that they would eventually be conquered by the Babylonians rather than by the Assyrians, who were then the great aggressive power. In our present section, the prophet turned his attention away from the nation as a whole, which was refusing to hear his message, and directed his words to the godly people of his day. These people, hearing his declaration of coming exile and knowing that as members of the nation they themselves were implicated in its sin, saw exile as certain, and might have been inclined to give way to despair. In chapters 40 to 56 Isaiah brought comfort to the godly of his day, assuring them that exile would not last forever, but God would deliver His people and bring them back to their homeland.

Although Isaiah had his contemporaries primarily in mind and sought to bring comfort to them as they imagined that the terrible Exile was already present, the Lord led him in such a way that his words would exactly meet the needs of the generation that would live in Babylonia one hundred and fifty years later, when it looked as if their captivity would never end. Isaiah's followers, knowing that his prophecies were sure to be fulfilled, would easily imagine themselves as already in this

19

situation. When the situation arrived and the exiles were suffering captivity and fervently longing for deliverance, they would read what Isaiah had written and would find that his words exactly met their needs.

This does not require us to assume that God simply dictated words to Isaiah without much personal thought or understanding on the part of the prophet. The situation of exile was very real to Isaiah. It was during his lifetime that the Northern Kingdom, which included two-thirds of the Israelites, was taken off into exile. Refugees must have escaped from time to time and brought news to the people in Judah about the sad fate of their northern brothers. Over and over, in earlier portions of his book, Isaiah predicted that Judah also would go into exile, and pointed out that the nature of its sin was such that any other result was clearly impossible. God could hardly leave the backsliding of His people unpunished.

It is one thing to talk about the troubles of a distant nation. It is quite another to look at your own people and know that they are headed toward misery and suffering. Not only would Isaiah have felt this way; the many godly in Judah who considered Isaiah a true prophet and accepted his words as coming from God Himself knew without doubt that terrible suffering and exile lay ahead. In these circumstances Isaiah brought them a message of comfort and deliverance. Awareness of the importance of this exilic situation in our present section is a prerequisite to understanding the section as a whole. Unless one has this background in mind, verse after verse is obscure and meaningless.

At this point we will glance at a few of the many verses in which exile is assumed and deliverance promised.

Isaiah 42:22 gives a vivid description of the situation of individuals in captivity:

> But this is a people robbed and despoiled; they are all trapped in caves or hidden away in prisons. They have become a prey with no one to rescue them, and a spoil with no one to say, Give them back.

Isaiah 44:28 assumes a situation in which Jerusalem has been destroyed:

> Who says of Cyrus, he is my shepherd and he shall perform all my desire; saying of Jerusalem, she will be built, and of the temple, your foundations will be laid.

Isaiah 45:13 includes the words:

> He will build my city, and he will set my exiles free, not for price or reward, says the LORD of hosts.

Isaiah 46:1 speaks of the fate of the people who would take Judah into captivity. This theme is continued in 47:1-5. Isaiah 47:6 declares that it was God who sent His people into exile, but rebukes the oppressors for showing them no mercy. Isaiah 48:14 declares that God will show His great love for His people by punishing Babylon.

Isaiah 48:20 presents in poetic form one of the clearest statements of God's intention to deliver His people from Babylonian exile:

> Go forth from Babylon! Flee from the Chaldeans! Declare this with joyful shouting, proclaim this, send it out to the end of the earth; say, The LORD has redeemed his servant Jacob.

Isaiah 51:14 reads:

> The captive exile will soon be released and will not die in the dungeon, neither shall his bread fail.

Isaiah 51:17 promises deliverance to a suffering Jerusalem:

> Rouse yourself! rouse yourself! Arise, O Jerusalem, you who have drunk from the LORD's hand the cup of his anger; you have drunk the cup of trembling; you have drained it out.

Isaiah 52:1-4 is a declaration that Jerusalem will be delivered from captivity and that its people will return. This promise of deliverance from exile reaches a great climax in verses 9-12:

> (9) Break forth into joy, sing together, you waste places of Jerusalem: for the LORD has comforted his people, he has re-

deemed Jerusalem. (10) The LORD has bared his holy arm before the eyes of all the nations; and all the ends of the earth will see the salvation of our God. (11) Depart, depart, go out from there, touch no unclean thing; go out from her midst, purify yourselves, you who carry the vessels of the LORD. (12) For you shall not go out in haste, nor go by flight: for the LORD will go before you, and the God of Israel will be your rear guard.

These quotations show clearly that Isaiah was writing for people to whom exile was a vivid reality. His words would first be read by his godly followers who imagined the situation as already present. They would bring even greater comfort and assurance to those who lived in exile over a century later.

# 3

## The King of Persia as Deliverer

THE GREATEST SUBJECT in this section of Isaiah is the coming of the One who will deliver His people and reestablish Jerusalem as the center from which His blessing will go out to all the world. The promises about this Messiah have been a great element in Jewish thought through the ages. The Dead Sea Scrolls frequently refer to the promised coming of the Messiah. At the beginning of the present century many Jews opposed Zionism, declaring that Jerusalem would not be reestablished and the Temple rebuilt until the Messiah would come. Yet the Hebrew word that is transliterated as "Messiah" occurs only once in the book of Isaiah, and in that instance it refers not to the Saviour but to a king of Persia.

Although this word occurs about forty times in the Old Testament most English versions render it as "Messiah" in only two of them (Dan 9:25-26). In all its other occurrences they translate it as "anointed," or "the anointed one." Occasionally it is used of a prophet, frequently of a priest, and most often of an Israelite king. Originally it meant one on whose head oil had been poured to indicate that he was set apart for a position to which God had called him. In a number of cases it is used of individuals who did not receive an actual anointing, so it is clear that the word came to mean simply one set apart by God for a special work. In its only use in Isaiah it designates a king of Persia as one appointed by God to perform the great accomplishment of delivering God's people from the Babylonian Exile.

As we have noticed, a great part of the material from Isaiah 40 to 52 deals with the problem of deliverance from exile.

### The King of Persia as Deliverer

It is natural to expect that the prophecy would give some idea of the human instrument God would use in providing this deliverance. In Isaiah 44:28 and 45:1 the human deliverer is designated by the name *Cyrus*. God declares that He will enable Cyrus to overcome all obstacles and to cause Jerusalem to be rebuilt and the foundation of the Temple to be laid.

As a young man, Cyrus ruled Persia. *Persia*, at that time, designated a small area in the southern portion of the territory dominated by the Medes. While still fairly young, Cyrus gained independence from the Median overlord and then was able to subdue him and to bring all the Medes under his control. Soon he led his armies westward through the territory north of the Babylonian Empire, conquering tribe after tribe. Turning still farther north, he entered Asia Minor. Here he defeated Croesus, king of Lydia, reputed to be the wealthiest man on earth. Following this victory, most of Asia Minor came under his control.

Cyrus's next step was to turn back and attack the empire of the Babylonians from the north. Again he was successful, and the city of Babylon itself fell to his soldiers and was made a part of his empire.

In his relation to the nations that had been held captive by the Assyrian and Babylonian oppressors, Cyrus reversed the policy followed by the previous conquerors. He tried to make the subject people feel that he was their friend, who had rescued them from Assyrian or Babylonian control. Thus he appeared to many nations as a deliverer, though he did not grant them independence or autonomy. Soon after his conquest of Babylon he gave permission to the Israelites and to other conquered peoples to return to their homelands. The first chapter of Ezra contains his decree permitting the Israelites to go back to Jerusalem and ordering that God's Temple be rebuilt.

After bringing the great Babylonian Empire under his control, Cyrus continued his conquests, turning eastward and conquering country after country. His successors rounded out his eastern conquests, including even Afghanistan and the north-western part of India. This vast region remained under Persian control for more than two centuries, until the Persian Empire was in turn conquered by Alexander the Great.

A number of passages in this section of Isaiah refer to Cyrus, although only two mention him by name. The first of these passages, 41:2-3, pictures the coming of a great conqueror from the east, whose appearance fills the nations with terror. The fact that Cyrus is not named until chapter 44, but is briefly described in earlier passages, is illustrative of a method of revelation that frequently occurs in the prophetic books, where a suggestion is first made or a situation briefly presented, and it is only later that the idea is enlarged and clarified, with further detail added. Practically all interpreters agree that these passages refer to Cyrus. The only important dissent is related to Isaiah 41:2-3, which is discussed in detail when chapter 41 is examined as a unit.

The second reference to Cyrus is in verse 25 of the same chapter, which reads:

> I have raised up one from the north, and he has come; from the rising of the sun he will call on my name; and he will come upon rulers as upon mortar, and as the potter treads clay.

Here God specifically claims that He Himself raised up a great conqueror. Although Cyrus came originally from the east, he conquered the regions north of Babylon before attacking that empire, so it is correct to say of him that he came from the north as well as "from the rising of the sun." The first chapter in the book of Ezra quotes the edict issued by Cyrus, in which he attributes his victories to the LORD and says that God has appointed him to build Him a house at Jerusalem (Ezra 1: 2). By making this edict, he certainly called upon the name of the true God, even if he never abandoned belief in other gods.

The latter part of the verse aptly describes the overwhelming power with which Cyrus conquered the nations.

The next reference to Cyrus is in the latter part of chapter 44, where he is specifically named in a long poetic sentence composed of a series of participial clauses describing God's activities and leading up to a promise that God will cause Jerusalem to be rebuilt and that Cyrus will be His shepherd to perform this task. This sentence begins after the first few words of verse 24. The translation below is so arranged as to show its logical structure.

> I, the LORD, am
>> the maker of all things, stretching out the heavens
>>> by myself and spreading out the earth
>>> all alone,
>> causing the omens of deceivers to fail, so that he
>>> makes fools out of diviners, causing
>>> wise men to draw back, so that their
>>> knowledge becomes foolishness,
>> confirming the word of his servant so that it fulfills
>>> the counsel of his messengers,
>> the one saying of Jerusalem, She shall be inhabited,
>>> and of the cities of Judah, They shall
>>> be built, and I will raise up her ruins,
>> the one saying to the deep, Be dried up, and I will
>>> make your rivers dry,
>> the one saying of Cyrus, He is my shepherd and he
>>> will perform all my desire, to say of
>>> Jerusalem, she shall be built, and of the
>>> temple, your foundation shall be laid.

This long sentence begins with an emphatic statement of God's creative power over the universe, followed by condemnation of false prophets and so-called wise men who wish to explain the universe without taking the Creator into account. Next God declares His determination to fulfill the predictions made by His messenger.

The first three parts of the sentence have stated general facts about God's activities, using a number of participles, none of which has an article attached to it. The three remaining parts predict specific future activities, each of them being introduced by the participle of the verb *to say* preceded by the definite article, and therefore meaning "the one saying" (or "the one who says"). Each of these three participles is to be understood as following the very first words of the sentence: "I, the LORD, am."

The first of these three final statements declares God's purpose to cause Jerusalem and the cities of Judah to be rebuilt, and the third specifically mentions Cyrus as God's shepherd through whom He will accomplish this purpose.

Verse 27, which comes between these two statements about God's purpose to cause Jerusalem to be rebuilt, might seem to repeat the idea of God's control over nature; but the context makes it rather clear that it means something quite different. Coming between the divine declaration that Jerusalem and the cities of Judah will be rebuilt (v. 26) and the statement that Cyrus will cause Jerusalem to be rebuilt (v. 28), it is reasonable to interpret both "the deep" and "thy rivers" as referring to the mighty Tigris and Euphrates rivers, which produced the fertile area in Mesopotamia and personified the conquering power of the Babylonian and Assyrian empires. In the context, the statement clearly means that the Babylonian power that destroyed Judah will itself be dried up.

For many centuries Mesopotamia had been a center from which conquering armies periodically marched out in various directions. After Cyrus's conquest, Babylon became merely a provincial capital and never regained its former greatness.

The word that we have translated as "the deep"[1] is sometimes rendered as "the depths of the sea," but this is a paraphrase rather than a translation. The word occurs only once in the Scripture, but a closely related word[2] is used not only for the depths of the sea but also to indicate a marsh or a river (as in Zechariah 10:11, where it refers to the Nile). The fact that it is used as parallel to "your rivers" in this verse strongly suggests that it refers to the land of the two rivers (Mesopotamia). However, some interpreters, preferring to take it as referring to the sea, note a few cases where *rivers* (or *streams*) also seems to point to the sea. In such a case, the verse is probably a reminder of the way God opened a path through the Red Sea to allow the Israelites to escape from Egyptian domination, and thus a figurative promise that He will remove the barriers to the rebuilding of Jerusalem caused by the existence of the powerful Babylonian Empire.

The prediction about Cyrus is continued in the first five verses of chapter 45.

> (1) Thus says the LORD to his anointed, to Cyrus, whom I have held by his right hand to subdue nations before him. I will loose the loins of kings, to open doors before him so that gates will not be shut. (2) I will go before you and make the rough places smooth. I will shatter bronze doors and cut iron bars, (3) and I will give you treasures of darkness and riches hidden in secret places, in order that you may know that it is I, the LORD, the God of Israel, who is calling you by your name. (4) For the sake of my servant Jacob and Israel, my chosen one, I have called you by your name. I have surnamed you, though you have not known me. (5) I am the LORD and there is no other; besides me there is no God. I will strengthen you, though you have not known me.

In 44:28 God called Cyrus His shepherd; in 45:1 He calls him His anointed (messiah). The LORD declares in these verses that He will give great honor and riches to Cyrus, enabling him to conquer powerful cities and overthrow mighty kings. Thus Cyrus is named as the one set apart by God to perform the great accomplishment of delivering God's people. The strong emphasis on the fact that God has called Cyrus by his name (vv. 3-4) implies that the prediction was given long before the Persian king became known. Verse 4 asserts that it was "for the sake of my servant Jacob, and Israel my chosen one," that Cyrus was called.

The words "though you have not known me," at the end of verse 4 and also of verse 5, imply that Cyrus did not realize that it was the God of Israel who enabled him to win his great victories.

Verse 13 of chapter 45 reads:

> I have raised him up in righteousness and I will direct all his

ways. He will build my city, and he will set my exiles free, not for price or reward, says the LORD of hosts.

The next passage that refers to Cyrus is Isaiah 46:11. It is introduced by a statement emphasizing God's power to accomplish what He chooses (46:10). Verse 11 reads:

Calling a bird of prey from the east, the man of my purpose from a far country. Surely I have spoken, surely I will cause him to come. I have purposed it; surely I will do it.

Calling Cyrus a bird of prey might seem quite contradictory to the King James translation of 41:2, which calls him "the righteous man from the east." As we shall see when we examine chapter 41, that phrase, more precisely translated "the man of righteousness from the east," is not a description of the character of Cyrus but a reference to what God would accomplish through him in establishing righteousness by working out God's just and holy plans. The figure of a bird of prey does not necessarily involve any criticism of Cyrus's moral character, but it is a very appropriate way of pointing out the nature of his career as one of constant conquest.

Before Cyrus conquered this great area, much of it was divided among various tribes or nations, each controlling a small region and often fighting against its neighbors. As a result of Cyrus's conquests, this whole area was integrated into a large region where individuals could travel more easily and within which the ordinary person could enjoy a far greater measure of freedom and opportunity for peaceful development than under the condition of having many small, independent sovereignties.

The final reference to Cyrus is in Isaiah 48:14-15:

(14) Assemble, all of you, and listen. Who among them has declared all these things? The LORD has loved him. He shall carry out his purpose on Babylon, and his arm shall be against the Chaldeans. (15) I, even I, have spoken; indeed I have called him, I have brought him, and he will make his way successful.

There has been some disagreement as to the reference of the

pronouns in verse 14. It is most reasonable to believe that the statement "the LORD has loved him" refers to the many ways that God had shown His love and mercy to Israel in days past. There is some disagreement among interpreters as to whether the next clause means that God will carry out His purpose against Babylon, or that Cyrus will carry out God's purpose against Babylon. But there can be little doubt that verse 15 refers to Cyrus, whom the LORD has brought forward and whom He will enable to succeed in his long career of conquest.

Thus the scattered statements about Cyrus bring out certain facts: (1) God raised up Cyrus for His own purposes; (2) the great successes of this Persian king, going beyond those of any known previous conqueror, are a vital part of God's plan; (3) the coming of Cyrus was predicted far in advance; (4) Cyrus is called God's messiah, since God set him apart for a specific work; (5) God's purpose in giving Cyrus his great successes was to make him His instrument for delivering Israel and causing Jerusalem to be rebuilt.

# 4

# The Symphonic Structure

WE HAVE ALREADY NOTICED a few examples of the great variety of material contained in this section of Isaiah. At many points, particularly in chapters 40 to 48, there seems to be a radical change of subject from one verse to the next. It may almost appear that the prophet simply dropped one subject and turned to an entirely different one. Then, after a verse or two, he left that for a third subject, then perhaps came back to the first or the second, and so on. These frequent transitions, often very sudden, are a marked feature of this part of the book.

The clue to the understanding of this is found right at the beginning of this section. Isaiah 40:1-2*a* literally reads, "Comfort my people, comfort my people, says your God. Speak to the heart of Jerusalem." The entire section might be called "Isaiah's Book of Comfort." Though he states important truths and describes wonderful acts that God will do in the future, his purpose is not simply to provide information. It is also to give comfort—to speak to the heart.

The construction of this part of Isaiah is somewhat like a symphony. A theme is presented and briefly discussed. Then a second theme is introduced which, in turn, may lead into a third. Again there is a felt need for reiteration of the first theme, then perhaps of the third again, and then of the second. Thus certain basic ideas are presented, repeated, and stressed, not merely to state the ideas they contain, important as this is, but to make a profound effect upon the hearts and minds of people who are already in their imagination suffering the horrors of the Babylonian Exile, which Isaiah had predicted (in Isa 39: 5-7) just before the beginning of this section of his book.

31

## The Symphonic Structure

We shall look at chapter 40 in detail a little later. At present we shall merely glance at a few of its verses as illustrating this important principle of symphonic structure.

The first five verses of chapter 40 look far beyond deliverance from exile, promising that the real cause of exile will be removed by the promised redemption from sin and predicting the work of John the Baptist. Verse 5 declares that the glory of the LORD will be revealed and all flesh will see it together. In the light of later understanding, it is easy to recognize that this looks forward to the incarnation; but the Israelites in the time of Isaiah might have taken it as promising a great manifestation of God's glory in the near future. Perhaps this declaration in verse 5 about the revelation of God's power and glory would arouse skepticism in the minds of many listeners. They would say to themselves: "Such promises are indeed wonderful, but look at the irresistible power of the Babylonian oppressors. See the great force that holds us in subjection! How can we believe that these things will actually occur?"

In answer, verses 6 and 8 proclaim the weakness of humanity and the shortness of human life. Human forces will wither, like the grass, but the Word of God will stand forever.

A similar transition occurs between verses 11 and 12. In verse 11 the Lord's gentle care for His people is beautifully described. Then it is as if the listener were to say: "These are wonderful promises. It is lovely to think of the Lord treating His people in this way, but we are faced with powerful enemies who are oppressing many nations. Can God actually do these things?"

In answer to this unexpressed objection, verses 12-17 stress the great power and wisdom of God. Compared to Him, all the forces of nature are tiny and insignificant. This theme of God's power occurs frequently in these chapters.

Verse 18 introduces a different theme, that of idolatry. Careless Israelites would be tempted to turn to the heathen rites of the Canaanites or to adopt the religion of their conquerors. Human nature often seeks an easy way to satisfy its religious needs without having to submit to God's moral law. In the first half of this section of Isaiah, a considerable amount of attention is given to condemnation of idol worship.

In our day idolatry seems like a relic of past times, yet we must recognize that the majority of those now living worship something other than the true God. All that is said against idolatry in our passage is highly relevant to our present situation if we substitute for the idol those other objectives or ideals to which modern men give the honor that is due the Creator.

Another theme that is important in this section of Isaiah is the theme of God's ability to predict the future. This important fact is stressed more in these chapters than almost anywhere else in the Bible.

In the early part of chapter 41 a new theme appears, that of "the Servant of the LORD." This theme is introduced so incidentally that it seems at first to be merely a part of other themes. Yet as the chapters go on, it is developed and stressed until eventually it becomes the most important element in this entire section of Isaiah.

As we examine succeeding chapters, we shall note many sudden transitions. Particularly sharp ones occur toward the end of chapters 42 and 43. Each of these chapters has a passage declaring God's promise to send great blessing (42:21; 43:19-21). In each case this is followed by a passage expressing great disappointment with His people and strongly criticizing them (42:22-25; 43:22-28). Then, as if the Lord feared that the words of condemnation might make His suffering people fall into utter despair, they are immediately followed by beautiful promises of indescribable blessing.

Without recognition of the importance of the symphonic structure, these chapters might seem like a patchwork of colors arranged in helter-skelter fashion. Once the underlying structure is recognized, they appear instead as a beautiful tapestry, with sections logically arranged in such a way as to convey great thoughts forcibly and yet tactfully.

# 5

## The Real Cause of Exile

THE PROPHETIC WRITINGS, including the other sections of Isaiah, frequently devote long passages to rebuking sin and predicting terrible punishment unless there is sincere repentance. Typical examples are found in Isaiah 1:2-23, 3:1-26, and 56:9—57:12. Yet the section with which we are dealing contains no lengthy passages of this type. This part of the book is written for people whose hearts are so filled with sorrow that direct rebuke might lead to despair.

Chapter 40 immediately follows the prediction at the end of chapter 39, in which Isaiah told King Hezekiah that the people of Judah would eventually be carried off into Babylonian captivity. Here the prophet addresses his followers, who realize the awful certainty that his predictions will be fulfilled. His present purpose is to bring them words of comfort. In so doing he gives a message that will be of particular help to the exiles more than a century and a half later.

While the apparent purpose of most of the early part of this section is to promise deliverance from exile, a more important purpose lies below the surface. Although sin is not often mentioned and rebuke is very rare in this section, a most fundamental part of Isaiah's purpose is to remind his listeners that sin is the real cause of exile and suffering. Unless something is done about the sin question, little will be accomplished by providing deliverance from exile.

Gradually the exiles are led to realize that deliverance from exile, important as it is, is not the final answer. The solution to the problem of sin is the greater need, and this section

34

of Isaiah reaches its climax in chapter 53, where God shows how He will solve that pressing problem.

This section of Isaiah contains a few short passages of stern rebuke, but they are preceded by longer passages of comfort, and they are usually presented not as a warning for the future but as an explanation of the reason for the Exile.

The Real Cause of Trials

...faith reaches the climax in chapter 27 where Paul shows
how He will bless each believer...

...

# The Great Overture

# 6

# The Importance and Uniqueness of Chapter 40

A STEADY DEVELOPMENT of thought begins in chapter 41. Here Cyrus suddenly appears, filling the nations with terror. God reassures the Israelites, telling them that Cyrus, instead of being a danger to them, is the divinely appointed instrument for their deliverance from Babylon. From this point the thought moves steadily forward, as God tactfully leads His people to realize that the Exile, terrible as it is, is only a symptom, and that the most vital problem is sin. Until this is removed any deliverance can be only temporary. Eventually complete deliverance from exile is declared and celebrated, and then the great deliverance from sin is presented and explained.

Before this steady progress of thought begins, there is a chapter that seems to stand by itself. Chapter 40 may be considered a beautiful overture to the entire section. It forms a definite unit, introducing the more specific prophecies that follow. It stresses the principal themes that will be developed in later chapters. As is quite natural in an overture, it starts at the end of the development rather than at its beginning. It pictures ultimate goals before reverting to consideration of the immediate situation.

Although it is not our purpose to examine every verse in this section of Isaiah but rather to stress the interconnections, to explain the great themes, and to show the development of thought, certain chapters are so important that they will be translated and presented in detail. One of the most important of these is chapter 40.

# 7

## Isaiah 40

Isaiah 40:1-5 reads:

> (1) Comfort my people, comfort my people, says your God.
> (2) Speak to the heart of Jerusalem, and proclaim to her, that
> her warfare is ended, that her iniquity is pardoned, that she has
> received from the LORD's hand double for all her sins. (3) A
> voice of one calling in the wilderness: "Prepare the way of the
> LORD, make straight in the desert a highway for our God."
> (4) Every valley shall be lifted up and every mountain and
> hill be made low; the rough ground shall become a plain, and
> the rugged terrain a broad valley. (5) And the glory of the
> LORD will be revealed and all flesh will see it together; for the
> mouth of the LORD has spoken.

The first word in this passage points to an important feature
of the entire section—the fundamental note of bringing comfort to people suffering misery as a result of their sins.

In the Hebrew, the words "my people" occur only once, but
a proper representation in modern English requires that they
be repeated, since the word "comfort" is in a form that indicates a transitive verb,[3] and therefore requires an object.

Verse 2 gives the command, "Speak to the heart of Jerusalem." The message is intended to reach the heart as well as the
mind.

In this verse it becomes evident that the victory over sin is
already in view. The proclamation clearly goes far beyond
anything that could be said to have been fulfilled by the return
from the Babylonian Exile. Its first phrase, "that her warfare
is ended [or, accomplished]," looks far beyond anything that
could be said to have happened when a comparatively small

part of the Jewish nation took advantage of the permission to return to Jerusalem granted by Cyrus after he conquered Babylon. About a century later, when Nehemiah was rebuilding the walls, he found it necessary always to be ready for active warfare. Still later, the great persecution under Antiochus Epiphanes led to the revolt of the Maccabees and a long period of constant warfare. It would be absurd to say that the promise of an end to her warfare (or, "hard service," if some would prefer that translation) merely pointed to the return from exile.

This is even more true of the next phrase, "that her iniquity is pardoned." The Bible nowhere teaches that Israel's guilt came to an end at the return from the Babylonian Exile.

The third phrase, "that she has received from the LORD's hand double for all her sins," would by itself be sufficient to show that this verse looks far beyond return from exile. In view of the biblical teaching about the terrible nature of sin, one could hardly think of the Exile, miserable as it was, as having been a complete expiation for all of Israel's sin, and there is no slightest hint in later portions of Isaiah that it could be so regarded. The proclamation clearly looks far beyond return from exile and points to the divine provision for atonement described so well in Isaiah 53.

Though there would seem to be little doubt of the general import of this third phrase, there have been some disagreements among commentators as to its exact sense, largely occasioned by the word "double," which gives rise to two apparent difficulties: (1) that it seems to present God as a tyrant who would exact double punishment for the sins of His people; and (2) that it suggests that sin is a matter of balancing punishment and wrongdoing in such a way that a man could completely pay the penalty for his sins; whereas the Bible teaches that sin is so terrible in nature that even the eternal suffering of a human being would be insufficient to pay a proper penalty for his sin.

A rather unusual interpretation has been the assumption that "double" here means "double blessing" and that the phrase is a promise that Israel would receive double blessing in spite of all her sins. Such an interpretation lacks philological justification, and there is no basis for introducing the idea of blessing into the word "double."

The solution to the difficulty lies in recognition that the Hebrew word used here,[4] one of several that are commonly translated "double," can properly be considered as similar to the English word "double" when used to represent a person who looks so much like another that it is difficult to distinguish them. Each of them is the "double" of the other, but neither is to be considered as equal to twice the other. It might be clearer to render it "equivalent," "counterpart," or "substitute." The phrase looks forward to the time when God will declare that the equivalent for the sin of all believers has been paid. No man could pay this penalty; only the divine Servant of the LORD could do it.

After the proclamation at the end of verse 2, it is natural to expect further detail. The following verses, while highly figurative in nature, aptly describe an important step in the great victory over sin. All four gospels take them as a prediction of John the Baptist. Luke 3:4-6 designates verses 3-5 as a description of his work and its results. The other three gospels quote John the Baptist as applying verses 3-4 to himself (Matt 3:3; Mark 1:2-3; John 1:23).

Those who have been raised on the King James Version do not realize how different an idea others might receive from the King James Version quotation: "the voice of one crying in the wilderness" (Luke 3:4). In modern English, *cry* generally conveys the idea of weeping. In these passages the word should be rendered "cry out," "cry aloud," "call," or "proclaim."

Verse 5 shows that the great climax of the redemption proclaimed in these verses is not a mere human deliverance but a vision of the glory of God which all kinds of people will see. Thus these verses look forward to the incarnation and are an appropriate introduction to the whole development described in Isaiah 41-56. So wonderful is the promise that a special attestation is given at the end of verse 5: "For the mouth of the LORD has spoken."

As the chapter goes on, it is easy to see in much of it the

reference to the great climax that our section reaches in its predictions of Christ in chapter 53. Yet there is very little in the chapter that is specifically connected with particular events, and in its latter part the center of attention seems to revert to the problems of the Exile.

(6) A voice is saying, Proclaim.⁵ Then he said, What shall I proclaim? All flesh is grass, and all its loveliness is like the flower of the field. (7) The grass withers, the flower fades when the breath of the LORD blows on it; surely the people are grass. (8) The grass withers, the flower fades, but the word of our God will stand forever.

The principle of "symphonic structure" is well illustrated by the sharp transition between verses 5 and 6. Perhaps the great declaration in verse 5 about the revelation of God's power and glory arouses a certain skepticism in the minds of some listeners. They say to themselves, How do we know that God will do these great things? In answer, a voice is ordered to call attention to human frailty. Man has his brief period of life and then, in most cases, is completely forgotten.

The Israelites in exile saw the great power of the Babylonians. All visible signs of God's existence and power had disappeared. The Temple had been destroyed. The walls of Jerusalem had been torn down. The people had been forcibly removed to places hundreds of miles away. A voice now declares that all this human power that looks so great is actually as weak as grass. When the LORD blows on it, it will disappear.

Today the site of ancient Babylon is almost devoid of people. Its greatness has vanished except in places where archaeologists have dug up some of the signs of its ancient glory.

Thus verses 6-8 emphasize the frailty of man and the fact that all his glory lasts only a limited time. In contrast, the end of verse 8 declares the permanence of God's Word.

(9) Get yourself up to a high mountain, O Zion, who brings good news; lift up your voice with strength, O Jerusalem, who brings good news: lift it up, do not fear; say to the cities of Judah, Behold your God! (10) See, the Lord GOD will come

with might, and his arm will rule for him. See, his reward is with him and his work[6] before him. (11) He will feed his flock like a shepherd, he will gather the lambs with his arm and carry them in his bosom, and will gently lead those that are with young.

The word "Zion," which is used eleven times in this section of Isaiah as a synonym for Jerusalem, was the name of the part of the city where David had built his palace.

Some interpreters take Zion and Jerusalem as being, like the cities of Judah, the recipients of the good news rather than those who brought it, since the common translation of verse 9 does not follow the order of the Hebrew words. There are strong arguments on both sides. In either case, the verse reiterates and stresses truths that are expressed in other parts of chapter 40 or in later chapters.

The good news proclaimed in verse 9 is elaborated in verses 10-11. God will show His mighty power to intervene in situations that have appeared hopeless. Not only will He do this, but He will do it with gentleness and love. He will feed His flock like a shepherd, and gather the lambs in His arms. This is a beautiful passage presenting God's love and mercy.

Between verse 11 and verse 12 there is a sharp transition. Verses 12-17 read as follows:

(12) Who has measured the waters in the hollow of his hand, marked off the heavens by the span, calculated the dust of the earth by the measure, and weighed the mountains in scales and the hills in a balance? (13) Who has directed the Spirit of the Lord, or instructed him as his counselor? (14) With whom did he take counsel? Who gave him discernment? Who instructed him in the path of justice, taught him knowledge, and showed him the way of understanding? (15) See, the nations are like a drop from a bucket, and are counted as a speck of dust on the scales. See! he lifts up the coastlands like fine dust, (16) and Lebanon is not sufficient to burn, nor its beasts enough for a burnt offering. (17) All the nations are as nothing before him; they are regarded by him as less than nothing and meaningless.

44

In answer to those who might find verses 10-11 difficult to believe, these verses lay stress on God's supremacy over nature. Verse 12 stresses His power in comparison with all the forces of the universe. Verses 13 and 14 emphasize God's infinite knowledge.

Scientists are constantly learning new facts about the tremendous complexity of God's creation. The human body is made up of separate cells, each of them a complicated organism in itself. There are so many of these cells that if those in a single body were placed an inch apart, they would reach many times around the earth. Each human eye contains more than half as many rods and cones as the total number of people in the United States. Botanists have discovered that the leaves on every tree are arranged in accordance with a mathematical formula. The more science advances, the more we can see how true are the words that the prophet cried out in verse 13: "Who has directed the Spirit of the LORD, or instructed him as his counselor?" When did God need to ask for advice in order to accomplish His work? Who would be capable of giving such advice?

Verses 15-17 again stress the greatness of God's power as compared to earthly forces. About 150 nations send their representatives to meetings of the United Nations. Yet all they can accomplish is like the small dust of the balance in comparison with God's power. He lifts up the great nations to the west of Israel as a very little thing. The term here translated "coastlands," or "isles,"[7] indicates any great area west of Palestine. Today it can include all the nations of Europe and of America. God can strengthen or can utterly wipe out any one of these "as a very little thing."

After verse 17 there is a transition to the closely related theme of the folly of idolatry. This transition is gradual rather than sharp, since the first part of verse 18 could be connected either with the verse before it or with those that follow.

(18) To whom then will you liken God? Or what likeness will you compare with him? (19) As to the idol, an artisan

must cast it, a goldsmith must plate it with gold, and a silver-smith must cast silver chains. (20) A poor man, unable to purchase such an offering, will select a tree that will not rot, and look for a skillful craftsman to prepare an idol that will not totter.

All through the early history of Israel, idolatry was a constant danger. This theme would become particularly important during the Babylonian Exile, where the Israelites often saw great processions honoring the Babylonian gods and giving them credit for enabling the Babylonians to conquer so large a territory.

In these verses Isaiah shows the folly of idolatry. The idols are simply made by men. Human intelligence, strength, and skill utilize materials that God has created. How foolish it is to worship what man himself has made!

In our day idolatry seems like a relic of past times, yet we must recognize that the majority of mankind today worship something other than the true God. All that is said against idolatry in our passage is highly relevant to our present situation if we substitute for "idol" those other objectives or ideals to which men give the honor that should belong to the Creator. A very common type of present idolatry is the worship of human intelligence or human science, which are really only finite efforts to understand the world that the infinite God has made.

Verses 21-22 again emphasize God's great power in contrast to the weakness of human substitutes for God.

(21) Do you not know? Will you not listen? Has it not been told you from the beginning? Have you not perceived the foundations of the earth? (22) He is the one who sits above the circle of the earth, to whom its inhabitants are like grass-hoppers. It is he who stretches out the heavens like a curtain and spreads them like a tent to dwell in. (23) He reduces princes to nothing and makes the judges of the earth meaningless. (24) Scarcely have they been planted, scarcely have they been sown, scarcely has their stem taken root in the earth, but he blows on them and they wither, and the storm carries them off like chaff.

The passage begins with a series of rhetorical questions, rebuking those who do not pay attention to the many evidences of God's existence and power. The final question asks, "Have you not perceived the foundations of the earth?" (Some translations insert the word *from* before "the foundations,"[8] but there is no preposition at this place in the original.) A man who looks at the great forces of nature and the complexity of the universe and fails to see the hand of the Creator is without excuse. The same idea is expressed by Paul in Romans 1:20, where he says, "The invisible things of him from the creation of the world are clearly seen, being understood by the things that are made, even his eternal power and Godhead; so that they are without excuse."

The next verse pictures God as sitting above the entire circle of the earth and stretching out the heavens like a tent. This is a beautiful figure, emphasizing the fact that God is everywhere and controls the entire universe.

Verses 23-24 go a step further. Not only has God power to overcome all human forces, but it is His intention to use this power. He declares that the great forces that seem so strong to the Israelites will wither and be blown away. In later chapters it is clearly predicted that the great power of Babylon will be demolished by the rising strength of Persia.

In verses 25-26 God again stresses His great power and declares that no one is equal to Him. Since He has created and controls all the forces of the universe, none of His plans can ever fail.

> (25) To whom then will you liken me, that I should be his equal? says the Holy One. (26) Lift up your eyes on high and see! Who created the stars? Who is the one who leads out their host by number, calling them all by name? Because of the greatness of his might, and the strength of his power, not one of them is missing.

As we have seen, most of verses 12-26 is related to the idea of God's greatness as compared to the weakness of humanity and the folly of idolatry. All this is relevant to the promise of the great victory over sin presented in the early verses of the chapter. Much of it is equally relevant to the immediate situation of the Israelites, with the inhabitants of the Northern Kingdom already in foreign exile and Isaiah's followers in the south knowing that their own kingdom will eventually suffer the same fate.

Beginning with verse 27, the LORD quotes and then answers the imagined complaint of the exiles, who are longing to be freed.

> (27) Why do you say, O Jacob, and declare, O Israel, My way is hidden from the LORD, and the justice due me is disregarded by my God? (28) Do you not know? Have you not heard? The LORD is the everlasting God. The Creator of the ends of the earth does not faint or grow tired. There is no searching of his understanding. (29) He gives power to the weary, and for those without vigor he increases strength. (30) Even youths may grow weary and tired, and young men may fall exhausted, but those who wait for the LORD will renew their strength; they will mount up with wings like eagles; they will run and not be weary; they will walk and not faint.

In verse 27 the LORD introduces the despairing cry of the exiles with the words, "Why do you say . . .?" Thus He suggests one of the basic questions of this whole section. Why should those who belong to so powerful a God complain? How can they even think that He would forget His people? He is the omniscient God, who needs no advice from human counselors. All wisdom, as well as all power, belongs to Him. We have surveyed the long statement of God's ability to destroy the ungodly forces that hold His people in subjection. Now He responds to Israel's complaint by renewed assurance that His great power can never fail and that His wisdom goes far beyond all human understanding.

We may pity the Israelites for needing such reassurance. Yet most Christians have similar times of doubt, and every believer can benefit from reading this passage.

Here, for the first time in the chapter, God calls Himself the Creator. Hitherto the emphasis has been mainly on His present power. Now He points back to the fact that He originated all that exists. He asserts that He can never become weary and that His understanding passes all human knowledge.

In the next three verses He promises that some of His endless strength will be imparted to His people. These verses should bring help and comfort to any believer who faces difficulties, but they must have had a very special meaning for the exiles.

Dragged from their homes and forced to live in areas hundreds of miles away, the exiles would think of the great distance between them and the land of Israel and would wonder how they could ever return. The thought of the long trip over difficult terrain would be enough to make even young men grow utterly weary. God promises that He will renew their strength. As they start their journey they will feel as if they are mounting up with wings as eagles. They will tend to run in their haste to get back to their homeland, but will not become as tired as might be expected. The climax is not reached in the sudden spurts, exhilarating as they may be, but in the ability to stick to the task until it is completed. Not only will they run and not grow weary; they will be able to continue the long walk and not become exhausted.

Chapter 40 ends in a way that would seem particularly related to the difficulties of returning from exile, and leads naturally into the succeeding chapters, where some of the immediate problems of the Exile are specifically discussed.

Part 1

# Babylon Overthrown and the Lord's Servant Introduced

# 8

## The Great Confrontation in Isaiah 41

THE CHAPTERS from 41-52, unlike chapter 40, contain specific names and deal with particular situations. In most of their contents the question of Israel's deliverance from exile is clearly involved.

As chapter 41 begins, God is imagined as addressing all the nations, including even the people of distant Greece ("coastlands," or "isles"), and calling upon them to recognize the powerful activities of the true God. While a cursory reading of verse 1 would make it appear that it is the people of the various nations who are being summoned to answer His charges, it will become apparent that His attack is particularly against their gods.

> (1) Keep silence before me, O coastlands: let the people renew their strength; let them speak; let us come near together to judgment. (2) Who raised up a man of righteousness from the east, called him to his foot, gave the nations before him, and made him rule over kings? He gave them as dust to his sword, and as wind-driven chaff to his bow. (3) He pursues them, passing on in safety, by a way that he had not entered with his feet. (4) Who has performed and accomplished it, calling the generations from the beginning? I, the LORD, the first, and with the last; I am he.

The summons in verse 1 is given in view of a specific situation which God claims to have brought into existence. The next verses describe the coming of a great conqueror whose activities strike fear into the hearts of many nations. Another reference to this conqueror occurs in verse 25, where practically all commentators agree that the reference is to the coming of

Cyrus, king of Persia. This chapter makes the tremendous claim that God is the One who brought Cyrus into existence and gave him the power to perform his great conquests.

Since Cyrus is not named until 44:28, a reader approaching 41:2-3 for the first time would have no clear indication of the identity of the person described if he did not read further. Recalling how Abraham rescued his nephew from the kings of the east (Gen 14), early Jewish interpreters suggested that Abraham is the conqueror mentioned here, and this opinion has been repeated by some later interpreters, including John Calvin and Matthew Henry. Yet as one reads further in the chapter, two facts become evident. (1) The coming of this conqueror causes many nations, including the distant "coastlands," to be filled with terror. This hardly fits the story of Abraham. (2) In verses 8-10 God exhorts the Israelites, whom He calls "the seed of Abraham," not to be similarly terrified. Such an exhortation would hardly fit with the idea that the conqueror just mentioned was Abraham himself, for a nation composed of his descendants could not exist until a much later time. It is interesting to note that even commentators who consider the person described in 41:2-3 to be Abraham interpret the later passages, including 41:25, as referring to Cyrus.

The idea that 41:2-3 refers to Abraham rather than to Cyrus may have been in part a result of a difficulty in the translation of the first clause of verse 2, which literally reads, "Who has raised up from the east righteousness?" The very early translation into Greek, called the Septuagint (translated about 200 B.C.), rendered the first part literally: "Who has raised up righteousness from the east?" As the following clauses obviously refer to a man, this clause has often been translated, "Who raised up the righteous man from the east?" This is the translation found in the King James Version, where "man" is printed in italics to show that it is an insertion. Since the original contains the noun *righteousness* (*ṣedheq*) rather than the adjective *righteous* (*ṣaddīq*), this is a rather free translation. If the word *man* is to be inserted it would be more logical to place it be-

54

fore "righteousness," making it read, "a man of righteousness." While this could describe a man who is righteous, it could equally well mean one who is God's instrument for accomplishing His own righteous purposes. Thus there is not necessarily any statement here regarding the character of Cyrus but rather regarding God's purpose in enabling Cyrus to carry on his great career of conquest.

When the verse is read exactly as it stands, it says that God is bringing His righteous and just purposes to fulfillment through one whom He will enable to make great conquests. It briefly introduces the conqueror from the east and declares that God has raised him up for God's own purposes.

Verses 5-7 describe the terror of the nations as they see Cyrus advancing. Their immediate impulse is to look for supernatural help, which they foolishly think can be obtained by preparing new idols.

> (5) The coastlands saw it and feared; the ends of the earth were afraid. They drew near and came. (6) Everyone helps his neighbor, and says to his brother, be strong. (7) So the carpenter encourages the goldsmith, and the one who smooths metal with the hammer encourages the one who beats the anvil, saying of the soldering, It is good; and he fastens it with nails so that it should not totter.

After this picture of the terror of the nations as they see the advance of the mighty conqueror from the east, a long passage is devoted to telling Israel why she need not similarly fear.

> (8) But you, Israel, are my servant, Jacob whom I have chosen, the descendant of Abraham my friend. (9) You whom I have taken from the ends of the earth, and called from its remotest parts, and said to you, You are my servant, I have chosen you and not rejected you. (10) Do not fear, for I am with you; do not be dismayed, for I am your God. I will strengthen you, indeed I will help you, indeed I will uphold you with my righteous right hand. (11) Behold, all who are angered at you will be put to shame and dishonored. Those who contend with you will be as nothing, and will perish. (12) You will seek those who contend with you, but will not find

them. Those who war with you will be as nothing, and non-existent. (13) For I am the LORD your God, who upholds your right hand. It is I who say to you, Do not fear, I will help you. (14) Do not fear, you worm Jacob, you men of Israel. I will help you, declares the LORD. Your redeemer is the Holy One of Israel. (15) See, I will make you a new sharp threshing sledge with double edges: you will thresh the mountains and crush them. You will make the hills like chaff. (16) You will winnow them, and the wind will carry them away, and the tempest will scatter them; but you will rejoice in the LORD; you will glory in the Holy One of Israel. (17) When the poor and needy seek water but there is none, and their tongue is parched with thirst, I the LORD will answer them; I the God of Israel will not forsake them. (18) I will open rivers on the bare heights, and springs in the middle of the valleys; I will make the wilderness a pool of water, and the dry land springs of water. (19) I will put in the wilderness the cedar, the acacia, and the myrtle, and the olive tree; I will set in the desert the juniper, together with the box tree and the cypress, (20) that they may see and know and consider and understand together, that the hand of the LORD has done this and that the Holy One of Israel has created it.

This beautiful passage presents a message of encouragement to the Israelites, assuring them that they are in an entirely different situation from the terrified heathen, since they have a special relation to the God who called Abraham His friend. This promise of blessing did not include all of Abraham's descendants but only those of the grandchild who was called "Jacob" in his early life and "Israel" later on. In verse 8 both names are used to represent all of Jacob's descendants. The Israelites are told that they need not fear, because God's blessing will continue with them. Even though in themselves they are so weak that He calls them a worm (v. 14), He declares that He will protect and strengthen them and will destroy their opponents.

The specific promises given in verses 11-12 have already been fulfilled to a very great extent. Most of the nations that oppressed Israel in ancient times have disappeared or been largely replaced. Assyria was demolished even before Judah was taken into captivity by the Babylonians. Babylonia was conquered by the Persians, then by the Greeks, then by Rome, and still later by the Arabs. Archaeologists study the remains of these great empires but see little in the present condition of these lands to suggest their ancient greatness.

Verses 17-19 contain beautiful pictures of the way God will bless His people, giving them abundant supplies of water. These statements would be particularly meaningful to people living in arid regions. Verse 19 describes a time when the wilderness will be changed into a beautiful garden—perhaps a glimpse of the time yet to come when all results of the curse will be removed (cf. Rom 8:18-23).

Verse 20 states the reason for all these blessings. They are given in order that Israel and all the nations of the world may see and understand the great power and goodness of God.

Immediately after these great promises to Israel, the LORD renews His challenge to the gods of the heathen.

> (21) Set forth your case, the LORD says. Bring your strong arguments, says the king of Jacob. (22) Let them bring them, and tell us what will happen; explain the former events, that we may consider them, and know their outcome; or let us hear what is coming. (23) Declare what will come hereafter, that we may know that you are gods; indeed, do good or do harm, that we may be dismayed as we observe it together. (24) Look, you are nothing, and your deeds are of no account. Whoever chooses you is an abomination.

The gods of the nations are challenged to predict the future or even to explain the meaning of the past. This challenge ends with an ironic assertion of the impotence of the heathen gods. The LORD declares that they do not even exist; they can do nothing, and all who follow them are utterly worthless.

This emphasis on the inability of heathen gods to predict the future points to one of the great themes of this section, the argument from fulfilled prophecy, which, like the emphasis on God's creative power, is stressed more often in this section of Isaiah than almost anywhere else in the Bible.

(25) I have raised up one from the north, and he has come; from the rising of the sun he will call on my name; and he will come upon rulers as upon mortar, and as the potter treads clay. (26) Who has declared this from the beginning, that we may know? or from former times, that we may say, He is right? Indeed, there is no one who declared it; indeed there is no one who proclaimed it; indeed there is no one who has heard your words. (27) In the beginning I said to Zion, See, here they are, and to Jerusalem, I will provide a bearer of good news. (28) But when I look, there is no man; there is no counselor among them who, if I would ask, could bring me word. (29) Behold, all of them are false. Their deeds are worthless. Their molten images are wind and confusion.

In continuing the divine condemnation of idols, these verses assert that it is the LORD who has raised up the great conqueror whose tremendous successes are vividly described in verse 25. No heathen god has foretold the meteoric rise of this tremendous historical figure. God has predicted these great events far in advance, but not a single one of the idols or soothsayers of the heathen has been able to do so. All of them are a mere delusion. Their deeds are worthless. Their idols are merely wind and confusion.

One additional matter in chapter 41 needs to be noticed. It is a subject that is given so little emphasis in this chapter that it could easily be passed over without any realization of its importance; but in succeeding chapters it proves to be one of the most important themes in the whole section. It was introduced in verses 8-9, where the prophet turned his attention to Israel to reassure them that they need not fear the aggressor who would so terrify their heathen conquerors. This reassurance was introduced by saying, "But you, Israel, are my servant, Jacob whom I have chosen." Verse 9 also includes the words "you are my servant." This beginning of a theme not previously mentioned, that of the Servant of the LORD, must be looked at more closely before examining the first stage of its fuller development in 42:1-7.

# 9

## The Servant of the Lord Introduced

THE TERM "Servant of the LORD" is familiar to everyone who is interested in the great Messianic passages of the book of Isaiah. The greatest Old Testament passage about the atonement, which runs from Isaiah 52:13 to the end of chapter 53, begins with the words, "Behold, my servant." Its next-to-last verse includes the statement, "By his knowledge shall my righteous servant justify many" (53:11).

This terminology does not begin with Isaiah 53. There is a long series of passages in this section of Isaiah in which such a phrase as "the LORD's servant" or "my servant" occurs. Chapters 42 and 49 each contain a long passage either describing this Servant or quoting his words. It is quite obvious that these two groups of verses are related to the long passage from Isaiah 52:13—53:12. As we shall see later, this section contains still another passage of several verses that should properly be placed in the same group.

The word *servant* is used far more in this section of Isaiah than in any other part of the book, and most of the instances seem to belong together. There is no verse in any other section of Isaiah that uses the word *servant* in a way similar to its use in these passages.[9] Thus it becomes evident that the idea of "the Servant of the LORD" is one of the outstanding themes in this part of Isaiah, briefly introduced in 41:8-9 and reaching its great climax in 52:13—53:12.

In the Old Testament, an idea is sometimes introduced by brief hints or incidental suggestions and then is later elaborated and clarified. After the entire revelation on a particular subject has been given, it may be possible to see that important aspects which did not become entirely clear until later passages were reached were already suggested in earlier ones. As we come to the passages dealing with this theme we shall examine each in its context, to determine its possibilities of meaning and to note how the thought develops.

When the term "my servant" first appears, in Isaiah 41:8-9, it refers to the nation of Israel. The context is very clear.* The surrounding peoples are filled with terror because a great conqueror is coming from the east. Cyrus is overwhelming country after country. The distant lands are terrified and begin to prepare new idols in order to find some hope of safety from this great aggressor who is making nations "like dust with his sword, like wind-driven chaff with his bow" (Isa 41:2). After vividly describing the terror of the nations in the aggressor's path, the LORD declares that Israel should not similarly fear, because Israel is His Servant whom He has chosen, whom He has taken from the ends of the earth and to whom He has said, "You are my servant."

This statement gives a very important insight into God's relation with Israel. God looks back to the time when He called Abraham to be the progenitor of the nation of Israel and explains the reason. He declares that it was not simply a matter of arbitrarily selecting one upon whom He would put His love, so that thereafter the Israelites could count on His protective care, no matter what they should do. God called Israel for a special purpose, in order that a certain work would be performed. Israel can know that it is God's Servant and that therefore God will preserve it.

There is no intimation given at this point as to the precise nature of the work that the Servant is to accomplish. Looking back, we know that Israel preserved the knowledge of the true God when most of the world had tried to forget Him. Israel produced the writers of most of the Old Testament books through which God gave His revelation to the world. These were great services. Yet as we examine the passages that discuss the work of the Servant, we shall see that they include ideas

*See p. 55.

60

that go far beyond these great services. The four longer passages, taken in conjunction with the extensive series of more or less incidental references to the LORD's Servant, show that in this part of Isaiah a very special concept is involved.

The first of these longer passages, which comes at the beginning of the next chapter (Isa 42), gives the very distinct impression that an individual is being described. Yet there are those who suggest that the term "the LORD's servant" in these chapters always represents the nation of Israel rather than one particular individual.

This contention cannot be lightly brushed aside, for many of the related passages seem to state it as a fact. Thus Isaiah 41:8 says: "But you, Israel, are my servant, Jacob whom I have chosen." Isaiah 44:1 reads: "Yet now hear, O Jacob my servant; and Israel, whom I have chosen." Isaiah 44:21 says: "Remember these, O Jacob and Israel, for you are my servant: I have formed you; you are my servant." Isaiah 45:4 says: "For the sake of Jacob my servant and Israel my chosen one." Isaiah 48:20 says: "The LORD has redeemed his servant Jacob." Isaiah 49:3 says: "You are my servant, Israel."

Does "the LORD's Servant" mean the nation of Israel, or does the phrase indicate a specific individual? At first sight the two statements would seem to contradict each other, so that if one were true the other would have to be false. Yet on closer examination we find that both can be considered true, since the idea may be viewed from two different sides, that of responsibility and that of accomplishment.

From the viewpoint of responsibility, the Servant of the LORD is the entire nation of Israel. God called Israel in order that Israel might be His Servant to do a particular work. In this first aspect all Israelites are included. Even if they are wicked, even if they turn their backs completely on the LORD, even if they have no desire to fulfill His will in any way—still the responsibility rests upon them, since it is for this purpose that God called Abraham in the first place. It is for this purpose that He protected Jacob. It is for this purpose that He made Jacob's descendants into a great nation and preserved it through the years. From the viewpoint of responsibility, the entire nation of Israel is God's Servant.

Second, however, there is the aspect of accomplishment. Like all nations, Israel included all sorts of people, both good and bad. As we read through the Old Testament, we find a great amount of denunciation of those Israelites who were wicked. Such individuals could hardly share in the accomplishment of God's work. How large a part of Israel is to be considered a part of the Servant who will actually perform the work? Will the fulfillment of Israel's responsibility involve nine-tenths of the nation? Will it involve half of the nation? Will it involve a fourth of the nation? Or is it even possible that the great work for which God has called Israel into existence is actually to be done by one individual, who is himself an Israelite and therefore can represent the nation in the fulfillment of the task? Answers to these questions become clear as the concept of the Servant is gradually developed and clarified in later passages.

Thus it is altogether proper to speak of Israel as the Servant of the LORD, because Israel has the responsibility to carry out the work of the Servant. Yet one must keep in mind the possibility that careful examination of the passages will show that, when it comes to accomplishment, the term describes a remarkable individual; he is himself an Israelite, so that he can represent Israel in fulfilling its responsibility, yet he possesses characteristics that could not conceivably describe an entire nation. Where responsibility is in mind, the term may describe Israel. Where accomplishment is in mind, each passage must be examined in order to determine whether there emerges a picture of a large group of people or of an individual.

Although most of the references to the Servant of the LORD are rather short, there are a few passages of greater length. The first of these, which consists of the first seven verses of Isaiah 42, will be examined in our next chapter.

# 10

## The Worldwide Work of the Lord's Servant: Isaiah 42:1-7

THERE IS A STRIKING CONTRAST between the end of chapter 41 and the beginning of chapter 42. Isaiah 41 ends with a strong condemnation of the idols. The false gods are nothing: they are merely wind and confusion. In contrast, chapter 42 begins with a picture of One who will exert power to a greater extent than any of the earth's great conquerors. His authority will be worldwide. "He will bring forth justice to the nations" (v. 1). He will "establish justice in the earth, and the isles will wait for his law" (v. 4). The entire passage reads:

> (1) See my servant, whom I uphold; my chosen one, in whom my soul delights: I have put my spirit upon him; he shall bring forth justice to the nations. (2) He shall not cry out or raise his voice or cause his voice to be heard in the street. (3) He will not break a bruised reed nor will he extinguish a dimly burning wick. But he will make justice come forth in accordance with truth. (4) He will not fail nor be discouraged till he has established justice in the earth, and the coastlands will wait for his law. (5) Thus says God the LORD, who created the heavens and stretched them out, who spread out the earth and what it produces, who gives breath to the people on it and spirit to those who who traverse it. (6) I am the LORD, I have called you in righteousness: I will hold you by the hand and guard you; I will make you as a covenant to a people, as a light to nations, (7) to open blind eyes, to bring out prisoners from the dungeon and those who sit in darkness from the prison.

The passage naturally divides into two parts, one of four verses and the other of three.

Unlike the first reference to the Servant of the LORD (41:8-9), which seemed to be merely an explanation of the reason Israel could be sure that it would be preserved, this passage appears to describe a person. The immediate impression is that it is a description of an individual rather than of an entire nation.

However, this by no means settles the question. Personification is frequent in the Scriptures. The nation of Israel is often personified and referred to by the name of its great ancestor, Israel, or even by his earlier name, Jacob, as in Isaiah 41:8, 14; 44:1-2, 21; 45:4; 48:20. At this point in our investigation, we cannot rule out the possibility that a nation is being described but shall merely notice that the passage gives the general impression of referring to an individual.

The passage deals principally with four main thoughts. The first is the assurance that God will so watch over and empower the Servant that there can be no doubt that his work will be accomplished. The second is a brief statement of the nature of the work that the Servant is to accomplish. The third is the gentleness with which the Servant will accomplish his work. The fourth is the confidence and apparent ease with which the Servant will move forward to perform his tremendous task.

All four of these thoughts are brought out in the first four verses. Some of them are again stressed or further developed in the last three verses of the passage.

The first thought is contained in the very first verse, which declares that God upholds His Servant, that His soul delights in him, that He has put His Spirit upon him, and that as a result the assigned task will be accomplished. Thus our passage is not a presentation of something that ought to be done but of something that definitely will occur. It is not an exhortation but a prediction. Verse 4 declares that the Servant will not fail or be discouraged until the work has been accomplished.

The second subject is the nature of the work that the Servant is to accomplish. Chapter 41 gave no information concerning the task for which Israel had been called to be God's Servant. In chapter 42 the task is only generally outlined; few details are given, and many aspects that are later developed are not mentioned here. The parts of his work stressed in these verses bear a close relation to the various matters described in the previous chapter. There the nations were filled with fear at the coming of a great conqueror whose purposes were quite unknown to them, though Israel was told that she need not fear this conqueror. Here it is stated that the Servant of the LORD will bring forth justice to the nations.

The word translated "judgment"[10] in the King James Version really means "the establishment of justice." The word there translated "gentiles"[11] can equally well be translated "nations." It covers all the nations outside of Israel and is sometimes used to include Israel as well.

This thought is repeated in verse 3: "He will make justice come forth in accordance with truth." These two verses show clearly that all injustice and wickedness are to be brought to an end by his activity, and that the justice that he establishes will be completely equitable and right. Further assurance that the Servant will establish complete justice throughout the earth is repeated in verse 4, with the added mention that the distant areas, which are called by the general term "coastlands," will wait for his law. Their actions will be controlled by his decision and they will look with expectation to his proper determination in all matters of uncertainty.

Thus in chapter 42 it is declared that the Servant will produce results that are worldwide in scope. The work is described in rather general terms, and, as we shall see later, some of the most vital aspects of the task of the Servant are not mentioned at all in this introductory passage.

In neighboring portions of this section of Isaiah much is said about the sad condition of the Israelites, held in captivity far from their homeland, tending to give way to despair, needing many words of comfort and hope. In our present passage the need of Israel is hardly touched upon. Attention is focused almost entirely on the tremendous task to be performed for the

Gentile nations, bringing judgment and law to the distant coast-lands.

The third and fourth subjects in the passage deal with the way the Servant will do his work. Here these matters are developed much more fully than the actual nature of the work. The second verse stresses the calm certainty with which he proceeds to accomplish his purposes. It is not necessary for him to exert great force. He does not face a crisis situation in which it is necessary to yell and push. He does not cry out or lift up his voice or cause it to be heard in the street.

Verse 2, taken by itself, could picture a supine, ineffective individual who was accomplishing nothing; but in connection with the great deeds summarized in the neighboring verses, it is clearly a picture of one moving forward with confidence, possessing such great strength that only a small part of it needs to be exerted to bring about the desired result.

Verse 3 further stresses the gentleness of his activity. It is not necessary for him to strike out violently, letting the chips fall where they may. He is so strong and so confident that he can deal gently and reasonably with every particular factor. He will not break a bruised reed that seems fit only to be thrown away. The same idea is brought out in the next figure: He will not "extinguish a dimly burning wick." The picture here is of a lamp that is trying to give light but failing to dispel the darkness. The natural tendency is to say, "Let's simply throw it away." He, however, will not quench it but will act gently toward it, giving it full credit for its effort. Thus verse 3 presents both his gentleness and his unfailing confidence.

This fourth factor, the confidence and apparent ease with which he will accomplish his task, is clearly brought out in verse 4.

These four verses contain a remarkable picture of the work the Servant will accomplish and the amazing manner in which he will perform it. It is no wonder that the mind cries out, after reading them, for assurance that there is a God who is able and willing to make this prediction come true.

In answer to this need, verse 5 departs from the immediate

subject and gives further assurance. Impossible as it may seem that the predictions contained in the first four verses will be fulfilled, we need not fear, for God the LORD has given His word. As evidence that what has been said will actually happen, the LORD points to the stupendous acts that He has already performed. It was He who created the entire universe. He established the wide reaches of space and determined the motions of the planets in their orbits. All the universe moves in accordance with His will.

From the declaration of God's power in making the universe as a whole, the verse proceeds logically to what He has done on this earth. Each of its features exists because it is His will that it should. In addition to the varied shape of the earth's surface, as He "spread it out," He formed all that it produces. All plant and animal life comes into existence according to His will.

Next the verse looks at human beings and declares that it is God who enables them to breathe. He gives spirit to those who traverse the earth. The human body without a spirit would be like an animal, greatly limited in every way and merely following its instincts, active for a few years and then forever still. God has placed everlasting spirits within human bodies. Every spirit comes from Him.

Thus verse 5 stresses the supreme power of God, as evidence that He can enable His Servant to perform all that has been stated in verses 1-4, and it also introduces the next two verses, which reiterate and amplify the first two factors already mentioned in verses 1-4.

The first factor is reiterated at the beginning of verse 6, as God asserts that He has called the Servant in accordance with His righteous purpose and will guard him as he performs his work. The second is discussed in the long sentence that begins in the latter part of verse 6 and includes all of verse 7. This sentence gives a new summary of the Servant's task. He will not be simply a military conqueror who treads down whatever is in his way. He is to be as a covenant to a people and as a light to nations.

The title "Servant of the LORD" is never applied to Cyrus,

who is described at several places in this section of Isaiah as an instrument for the accomplishment of God's purposes. God declares that He will give Cyrus great victories, and even calls him His anointed one (Heb., *messiah*), but never speaks of him as the LORD's Servant. In this part of Isaiah the word *servant* is restricted almost entirely to a specific one who is described in this and later passages.

Although there is no mention of sin in this passage, there is a reference to its effects. Verse 7 shows that the work of the Servant involves alleviation of the misery that sin has produced. He will open blind eyes and bring out prisoners from their dungeons.

There is no mention in these last two verses of the way that the Servant will do his work, this having been rather fully discussed in the first four verses.

In these seven verses the emphasis is on the worldwide work of the Servant. Much is said of what He will do for the nations and for the distant coastlands, but there is no clear statement that He will do a work for Israel. Only by inference can it here be suggested that since Israel is blind it will be necessary to open her eyes, or that since Israel is in prison it will be necessary to free her.

Release of Israel from exile might be thought of as involved in these verses, but there is here no specific statement connecting Israel's return from exile with the work of the Servant. In fact, apart from one rather uncertain phrase, there is no specific statement in this passage about the Servant doing anything for Israel. The one phrase that might be thought of as referring exclusively to Israel is found in verse 6, which says, "I will make you as a covenant to a people, as a light to nations." Here the phrase "covenant to a people" could be taken as referring to Israel in contrast to the nations to which the Servant is to bring light. Yet it is equally possible to consider it as a general statement that the Servant will represent God's covenant to each of the various nations. In the light of New Testament teaching it would certainly be possible to take it as referring to His covenant with all who are saved through the work of the Servant.

The emphasis of the passage is on what is to be done for the nations, and this could fit well with the idea suggested by the language of Isaiah 41:8-9, that the Servant is the nation of Israel. Yet a contrary suggestion flows naturally from the statement about the way the work is to be done (vv. 3-4), with its picture of gentle strength and confidence, quite contrary to the usual impression given by the nation of Israel or by the average Israelite. It is hard to reconcile this description with the idea that Israel is the Servant here described.

An Israelite reading this passage for the first time might well stagger in an attempt to comprehend it. In chapter 41 he learned that God had called his nation to do a great task. In this passage he learns that the task involves bringing justice and light to all the nations of the earth. He remembers how the mighty King David conquered the nations immediately north and east of Israel and established a sizable empire, bringing a measure of justice and light to quite a few nations. But even David's empire was small compared to the great empires of Egypt and Assyria. This picture goes far beyond what David accomplished. It includes even the distant "coastlands." Moreover, in Isaiah's time Israel was far weaker than it had been in David's time. The nation had been broken into two parts, and during Isaiah's lifetime the northern and larger portion was conquered and transported into captivity far across the desert. It would take a great exercise of imagination to think that the small nation of Israel could conquer the whole world, as David had conquered the nations in his area, and would be able by this means to bring justice and light to all people. Thus far, the problem of interpretation is already extremely difficult; but when the Israelite reads verses 2-3 and learns that all this is to be accomplished without calling out or even lifting the voice, with the gentleness and patience that are described in verse 3, and with the utter lack of hesitation or discouragement that verse 4 demands, he will surely throw up his hands and confess that he cannot understand how Israel can possibly fulfill these verses.

After reading in chapter 41 that God will deliver Israel because Israel is God's Servant, and then reading the description in chapter 42 of the work that God's Servant must do, an Israelite might easily be filled with skepticism and wonder. How could Israel, in bondage, in weakness, and in suffering, bring justice to the Gentiles? How could Israel, with its little strength, go forward with such tremendous power that it would not need to raise its voice or to break the bruised reeds?

Feeling its utter inability to perform the work assigned to the Servant of the LORD, Israel might well think that the figures of the bruised reed and the dimly burning wick meant Israel itself. Israel, which should be a strong force to accomplish the work for which God called it into the world, is broken by oppression and exile and is suffering the result of its sin. Israel, which should be a bright light to show forth the truth of God's Word, is merely a smoking wick. God promises that the Servant will not cast aside or throw away this instrument.

An unthinking Israelite who reads the passage might consider that in some way this description of the Servant pictures what Israel will actually succeed in doing. But a more discerning Israelite might conclude that the Servant described in chapter 42 is a wonderful figure sent by God to do God's work and would therefore give thanks that the Servant will deal gently with Israel instead of casting it utterly aside for its failure and sin.

If the revelation about the Servant of the LORD stopped here, so that nothing was known about him beyond the fact that the term is applied to Israel in chapter 41 and that his work and character are thus described in chapter 42, reconciliation of the two would be a very difficult problem. Fortunately the subject is greatly developed by the prophet in later chapters.

# 11

## A Picture of Frustration: Isaiah 42:8-25

AFTER THE BEAUTIFUL PICTURE of the gentle but supremely effective work of the Servant in 42:1-7, the remainder of the chapter includes a number of very striking transitions. Yet there is a definite progress of thought leading to the terrible frustration that is described in the last fourth of the chapter.

> (8) I am the LORD, that is my name. I will not give my glory to another, nor my praise to graven images. (9) See, the former things have come to pass; now I declare new things. Before they spring forth I am informing you of them.

Verse 8 might be thought of as parallel to verse 5 and therefore as an assurance that the powerful God will make sure the work assigned to His Servant will actually be accomplished. Yet this verse does not, as does verse 5, emphasize His power over nature. It merely declares that He will not give His glory to anyone else or His praise to idols. Therefore it seems best to consider it the beginning of a new paragraph rather than a continuation of the previous passage.

This assurance of God's unique position can easily raise in the mind of the listener a question as to how one can know that it is true, since all visible signs of God's power will have perished in the destruction of Jerusalem. Again, as so many times in this section of Isaiah, the answer is given by a reference to God's ability to predict the future. He declares that the exiles can already see how precisely His former predictions have been fulfilled, and He promises to give additional predictions of events yet to come (v. 9).

**71**

After these assurances the prophet breaks forth into song and gives a wonderful doxology in verses 10-12.

> (10) Sing to the LORD a new song; sing his praise from the end of the earth, you who go down to the sea, and its fullness, the coastlands, and all their inhabitants. (11) Let the wilderness and its cities lift up their voice, the villages that Kedar inhabits. Let the inhabitants of Sela sing for joy, let them shout from the top of the mountains. (12) Let them give glory to the LORD, and declare his praise in the coastlands.

In the next three verses the tenor of the passage is interrupted by some statements rarely paralleled in this section of Isaiah.

> (13) The LORD will go forth like a warrior. He will stir up his zeal like a man of war. He will utter a shout, he will raise a war cry. He will prevail against his enemies. (14) I have kept silent for a long time. I have kept still and restrained myself. Now I will cry out like a woman in travail; I will gasp and pant. (15) I will lay waste mountains and hills, and dry up all their vegetation. I will make the rivers islands, and I will dry up the pools.

In sharp contrast to the picture in verses 1-7 of the gentle and confident progress of the Servant's work, this passage describes a time when God will exert His divine power in violent fashion, destroying enemies and making great changes in the external world. The Servant described in verses 1-7 does not lift up his voice or cry, but here the prophet describes a time when God Himself will raise a war cry, utter a shout, and cry out like a woman in travail.

This passage can serve as a reminder that God's silence will not last forever. For a long time human ideas and desires may seem to prevail, and God's patience may be misinterpreted as proving that He does not exist; yet every now and then He exerts His power in violent and unexpected ways. Great cataclysms occur that leave the shape of the world quite different from what it was before. Many such changes have occurred in the world's history. Babylon was for many centuries one of the greatest powers in the world, and at the time of Judah's exile it seemed to be the strongest of them all. Yet the coming of Cyrus was to topple Babylon from its high position, and within a few centuries all that would remain would be some heaps of ruins.

(16) Then I will lead the blind by a way they did not know. I will guide them in paths they have not known. I will make darkness light before them and crooked places straight. I will do these things, and I will not forsake them.

The fact that the beautiful promises of verse 16 come directly after the picture of violent destructive action in verses 13-15 is evidence that those verses are directly related to the deliverance of the Israelites from Babylon rather than to the work of the Servant, so different in nature. Israel, blinded by her sin and suffering under Babylonian captivity, will be freed as a result of such violent occurrences as are figuratively described in verses 13-15. God will raise up a mighty conqueror who will destroy the Babylonian armies, tear down their defenses, and put an end to their empire. God will lead the blind by a way they do not know, making darkness light before them. Israel will be delivered as the result of a violent cataclysm that she herself has no part in producing.

(17) They shall be turned back and utterly put to shame, who trust in idols, who say to molten images, you are our gods. (18) Hear you deaf, and look you blind, that you may see.

Verse 17 shows the utter rout of the idols that seemed so powerful during the time of Israel's exile. All who trust in them will be put to shame.

Verse 18 is a transitional statement which some commentators connect with what precedes, while others consider it an introduction to what follows. It actually looks both ways. Those who are trusting in idols are told to open their eyes and see the truth about this foolish worship. Nature is filled with evidences of God's wisdom and power, which man tends blindly to ignore. God calls on everyone to see the evidences of the true God that are all around us.

Yet this statement of the folly of idol worship leads to consideration of the failure of those who should be God's own, whose blindness has already been mentioned in verse 16.

(19) Who is blind but my servant, or deaf, as my messenger whom I send? Who is blind as he that should be perfect, or so blind as the LORD's servant? (20) You have seen many things, but you do not observe; your ears have been opened, but no one listens.

After looking at the blindness of those trusting in idols, the prophet expresses amazement that anyone who has enjoyed the great privilege given to Israel should fail both to realize his responsibility and to recognize the true meaning of life. Terrible as it is that men should forsake the living God and trust imaginary beings that are not gods at all, it is even worse for those who have been given God's revelation to fail to live up to the responsibility that He has set before them.

Here it is declared that even the idol worshipers are not as blind as the LORD's Servant. This term was used twice in 41: 8-9 to show why God had called Israel in the first place, and thus to explain why He would never give them up. The statements in verse 19 might seem very difficult to reconcile with the declaration in verses 1-7 of this same chapter that the Servant will accomplish the work of bringing justice to all the nations, or with the description there of the manner in which He will perform this work. In order to reconcile the apparent contradiction, it is necessary to recognize that responsibility for the performance of the work rests upon the whole nation of Israel, even though its actual performance may require the divine selection and enduement of one particular individual. These verses lament the inability of Israel to perform the task, an inability that involves a definite failure to follow the LORD as she should.

Verse 19 consists of four statements, the first and last of which are almost identical. Blindness and deafness are attributed to the Servant, who is also called the messenger whom God has sent. It was an important part of Israel's function to witness to God's power. Israel was God's messenger to the world. The responsibility of the LORD's Servant rests upon Israel, and yet Israel is blind and deaf.

In the King James Version, the third phrase in verse 19 seems quite out of harmony with the others. It reads: "Who is blind as he that is perfect?" The rather rare form here translated "perfect" could be derived from either of two very similar Hebrew verbs, one of which means "to be whole, sound, or perfect."[12] The other means "to be at peace," or "to be in a covenant of peace."[13] The form of the verb is a passive *pual* participle.[14] There are a number of instances in Hebrew where certain types of passive participles are considered similar to the Latin gerundive, which indicates what ought to be rather than what is. If this interpretation is permissible here, it would fit perfectly with the context, and would designate one who ought to be perfect enough to do the work described in the early part of this chapter as the task of the Servant of the LORD. Another possible interpretation, deriving from the other root, would take it as meaning "one who has been placed in a covenant of peace."

Verse 20 continues the thought of verse 19 in somewhat elliptical fashion. The word that we have translated "observe" means "to keep, or guard." It does not mean that the Servant has not looked intelligently at the many things he has seen but rather that he has failed to carry out and protect God's commandments.

> (21) The LORD was pleased for his righteousness' sake to make the law great and glorious. (22) But this is a people robbed and despoiled; they are all trapped in caves or hidden away in prisons. They have become a prey with no one to rescue them, and a spoil with no one to say, Give them back. (23) Who among you will give ear to this? Who will give heed and listen for the time to come? (24) Who gave up Jacob to the spoiler, and Israel to the robbers? Was it not the LORD, against whom we have sinned? and in whose ways they would not walk, and whose law they did not obey? (25) Therefore he has poured on him the fury of his anger, and the might of battle. It set him on fire roundabout, but he did not understand it; it burned him, but he did not take it to heart.

Verse 21 might seem to represent a change in subject, but it is actually a reiteration of God's determination that the work of the Servant will be fulfilled and God's law made great and glorious by the One who will establish justice in the earth.

Verse 22 returns to the inability of the Servant to carry out this work. How can Israel bring justice to the nations and establish God's purposes throughout the world when the Israelites themselves are trapped in caves or hidden away as prisoners, with none to deliver them? How can Israel do the work of the Servant when Israel itself is in bondage?

In answer to this frustration, the prophet lashes out with the strongest words of condemnation for Israel's sin that our section has yet contained. He declares that God Himself has given Israel to the robbers because they sinned against Him and refused to walk in His ways and be obedient to His law. For this reason He has poured on Israel the fury of His anger. Yet even now, He says, Israel has not taken it to heart. Thus chapter 42, which began with complete confidence that the great work of the Servant would be accomplished, ends in utter frustration because of the inability of those who have the responsibility for fulfillment of this work. The reason for Israel's inability is shown to be Israel's sin. The problem has been made clear. It will be further emphasized and developed before the solution is reached.

# 12

## Isaiah 43

AFTER THE VIGOROUS DENUNCIATION of Israel with which chapter 42 ends, there is a very sharp transition. Chapter 43 begins with seven verses expressing in the strongest way God's great love for Israel and His determination to give her indescribable blessing in days to come.

(1) But now, thus says the LORD who created you, O Jacob, and he that formed you, O Israel: Do not fear, for I have redeemed you; I have called you by name; you are mine! (2) When you pass through the waters, I will be with you; and through the rivers, they will not overflow you. When you walk through fire, you will not be burned, and the flame will not scorch you. (3) For I am the LORD your God, the Holy One of Israel, your Saviour. I have given Egypt as your ransom, Ethiopia and Seba in your place. (4) Since you are precious in my sight and honored and I love you, I will give men in return for you and people in exchange for your life. (5) Do not fear, for I am with you. I will bring your offspring from the east and gather you from the west. I will say to the north, Give up, and to the south, Do not withhold. Bring my sons from afar and my daughters from the end of the earth, (7) everyone who is called by my name, whom I have created for my glory, whom I formed and made.

God begins by declaring that He is the One who has created and formed Israel. The second verb[15] suggests His control over the development of each of His creatures. Not only does existence begin as a result of His command; all the many elements that enter into the life of one of God's people are supervised and controlled by the Creator.

The verse continues, "Do not fear, for I have redeemed you." The Hebrew word translated "redeemed"[16] originally indicated a very definite concept, picturing the reclaiming of a person (Lev 25:48), an animal (Lev 27:13), or a piece of land (Lev 25:25; cf. Ruth 4:4-6) by making a payment or by providing a substitute.

Not only has God created Jacob and developed the nation, He is even ready to redeem it after it has been lost through its own sin. Despite the strong criticism leveled at Israel in the verses immediately preceding, deliverance from Babylon is here specifically promised.

The second verse follows naturally from the first. Even when God's redeemed people go through fiery trials, they can know that He is with them, to lead and to protect.

While these two verses relate primarily to Israel, they are equally applicable to every true believer, since each one is a special creation of God. God's creative power was necessary to turn us from darkness to light and from the power of Satan to the power of God.

All men have been lost through their sin and need to be redeemed. Everyone who has been redeemed through the penalty that Christ paid on the cross belongs forever to the LORD and should know that nothing can ever happen in his life without God's definite purpose. Therefore he has a right to take the words "do not fear" as a solemn command and a definite assurance that he should not fear anything that can happen to him in this life. God controls all things and makes them work together for His own purpose in the development of His people. This fact is vividly illustrated by the second verse, with its references to danger from flood and fire and its promise that God will protect His own—all those who are called by His name (v. 1).

Every Christian could be greatly blessed by taking to heart the meaning of these two verses. His problems would be greatly simplified if he would realize that God has created him, has formed him, and has redeemed him, and that therefore everything that comes into his life is part of God's plan and is ultimately intended for his good. When these facts are properly evaluated, there remains no excuse for the fear and anxiety that afflict many Christians. It is the right of everyone who belongs to the true God to lean upon Him and to know that the only thing that keeps us from enjoying His very best is our own sin and our tendency to wander from His love.

Verse 2 also makes it clear that God gives His people no assurance that there will not be great difficulties ahead of them. It is God's desire that His people be molded and formed in accordance with His will, and this sometimes requires the fires of affliction. These fires may be the result of one's own sin; they may be a by-product of the sins of others; or they may simply be part of the situation in which the Lord has chosen to place one. Whatever the explanation of a particular tribulation or suffering, the believer can always know that he would not have the experience if it were not God's will. He should realize that it is God's intention to bring him blessing through whatever affliction he may have to endure, and to use it as a means of molding him into the sort of person God desires him to be.

The verse assures us that when we have to pass through tribulation we need never do so alone. God will be with us when we pass through the waters. He will not suffer us to be tested beyond what we are able to bear. The rivers will not overflow us. They may seem very high, but they will never pass over our heads. Deadly fire may be all around us, but it cannot permanently injure us except in such a way as may be part of God's will for our good. Any Christian would do well to memorize these two verses and apply them to his life, even though in the context their primary application is to Israel, whom God brought into being for a very important purpose—a purpose that is the subject of this whole section of Isaiah.

In verse 3 the LORD's definite relation to Israel is again stressed, and He calls Himself her Saviour. The term *Saviour*[17] is applied specifically to Jesus Christ in the New Testament about sixteen times, and to God eight times. The corresponding Hebrew word[18] occurs seventeen times in the Old Testament (though the King James Version renders it as "saviour"

79

in only fifteen of these occurrences). In eleven of these Old Testament occurrences it refers to God. Five of the eleven are in our present section.

The last part of verse 3 has a more temporary significance. Most scholars agree that it refers to the fact that Cambyses, the son of Cyrus, would extend Cyrus's conquests to include Egypt, Ethiopia, and Sheba, and that Isaiah thinks of these added conquests as being a ransom to Cyrus for having permitted the Israelites to return to Jerusalem.

God's love to Israel, His erring people, continues to be stressed in verses 4-7. Here there is a note that has not previously occurred in our section, that of searching out His people wherever they may be scattered, whether to the east or to the west (v. 5) or to the north or to the south (v. 6), and bringing them back to their own land.

Some interpreters consider that this was not fulfilled in the return from the Babylonian Exile because then a comparatively small portion of the nation took advantage of Cyrus's permission to return to the land of Israel. They therefore believe that it relates to a future regathering in which all the Israelites will be brought back to Palestine. It is not within the purpose of the present writing to take a dogmatic stand on one side or the other of this question. In any case, a Christian is entitled to draw from these verses the lesson that no matter where he may wander, God still has His hand upon him. God desires to bring back to Himself everyone who comes under the category described in verse 7, which strikes a universal note. The blessing described here applies to everyone who is called by the LORD's name, who was created for His glory and belongs to Him.

> (8) Bring forth the people who are blind, yet have eyes, and those who are deaf, yet have ears. (9) Let all the nations be gathered together, and let the people be assembled. Who among them can declare this and explain to us the former things? Let them bring forth their witnesses, that they may be justified, or let them hear and say, It is true. (10) You are my witnesses, says the LORD, and my servant whom I have chosen,

in order that you may know and believe me, and understand that I am he. Before me no god was formed, and there will be none after me. (11) I, even I, am the LORD, and there is no saviour besides me. (12) I declared and saved and proclaimed, when there was no strange god among you; therefore you are my witnesses, says the LORD. I am God (13) and also from today I shall be he, and there is no one who can snatch you out from my hand. When I work, who can reverse it?

Verses 8-13 describe a confrontation similar to that in chapter 41. All the nations are gathered together, and their gods are challenged to explain the course of events. The LORD calls on them to present their witnesses. Then He turns to the Israelites and says: "You are my witnesses and my chosen servant." God raised up Israel to be witnesses to the truth of His Word. Almost alone of the people of antiquity, they have survived to this day. Scattered throughout the world, their very existence witnesses to the truth of the predictions of God's Word.

Most interpreters consider verse 8 as beginning the challenge to the idol worshipers. Very few think that it goes with the preceding section and refers to Israel.

In verse 9 there is a ringing challenge to the idols to prove that they are really gods, and the following four verses repeatedly stress the eternity of God and His existence as the only God.

The passage thus has two purposes: (1) to denounce the folly of worshiping idols, presenting Israel as a witness against it; and (2) to encourage the Israelites to be true to God and to follow Him.

> (14) Thus says the LORD your redeemer, the Holy One of Israel: On account of you I have sent to Babylon and will bring them all down as fugitives, even the Chaldeans, into the ships in which they rejoice.

Since verse 14 begins with a statement that God is the Redeemer of Israel and mentions Babylon, it is natural to interpret it as a prediction of the coming deliverance from Babylon, but its precise meaning is obscure. The word the King

James Version translates as "nobles"[19] is now more generally rendered "fugitives," but its meaning here remains uncertain. The leading group in Nebuchadnezzar's Babylon were called Chaldeans. Perhaps the verse contains an allusion to events or situations that are not at present known to us. In any event, its emphasis is clearly on the sovereign power of God in controlling history.

This leads naturally to continued emphasis on God's sovereign power in verses 15-17.

> (15) I am the LORD, your Holy One, the creator of Israel, your king. (16) Thus says the LORD, who makes a way through the sea and a path through the mighty waters, (17) who brings out chariot and horse, army and warrior. They will lie down together and not rise again. They have been extinguished like a wick.

Here the deliverance of the Israelites described in Exodus 14 is recalled. God reminds His people of the way He made a path through the Red Sea to allow their ancestors to escape from the Egyptian warriors with their chariots and horses, and of how He caused these oppressors to follow the Israelites into the sea, where they were overwhelmed by the returning waters, lying down, never to rise up again.

> (18) Do not remember the former things or consider things of the past. (19) See, I will do a new thing; now it will spring forth. Will you not perceive it? I will even make a roadway in the wilderness and rivers in the desert. (20) The beasts of the field will honor me, the jackals and the ostriches, for I have given water in the wilderness and rivers in the desert, to give drink to my chosen people.[20] (21) The people whom I formed for myself will declare my praise.

Great as were God's wonderful works for His people in the past, He promises that future blessings will be even greater. In order to enable them to return from Babylon to their homeland, He declares that He will make a roadway through the wilderness, with abundant water available and all nature honoring its Creator.

Verse 21 declares the purpose of all this. The people whom God formed for Himself are to declare His praise. Thus the chapter has laid great stress on the responsibility of Israel to be God's witness. It should make Him known to the ends of the earth as part of its responsibility toward fulfilling the work assigned to the LORD's Servant.

At this point there is a sudden sharp transition, paralleling the one near the end of the previous chapter. The declaration of God's wonderful blessings to Israel, which bears responsibility to fulfill the work of the Servant of the LORD, leads to recognition of the inability of the nation to fulfill the task.

> (22) But you have not called on me, O Jacob; but you have become weary of me, O Israel. (23) You have not brought me your sheep for burnt offering, or honored me with your sacrifices. I have not burdened you with offerings, nor wearied you with incense. (24) You have bought me no sweet cane with money. Neither have you filled me with the fat of your sacrifices. Instead you have burdened me with your sins; you have wearied me with your iniquities. (25) I, even I, am the one who blots out your transgressions for my own sake, and I will not remember your sins. (26) Put me in remembrance; let us argue together; state your case, that you may be proved right. (27) Your first forefather sinned, and your representatives have transgressed against me. (28) Therefore I will profane the princes of the sanctuary, and I will give over Jacob to the curse and Israel to reviling.

The first three verses in this passage are among the saddest in the Bible, as they show God's erring people failing to return His love, becoming weary of Him, and even burdening Him with their iniquities. The loving heart of God, saddened by the sin and waywardness of His people, never finds clearer expression than here. But the Christian should never consider this passage as merely an account of wayward Israel. All of us need to take these words to heart and realize how far short we come of showing true gratitude to God for all He has done for us.

Verse 25 must be taken as a prediction of the future. God promises that for His own sake He will blot out the transgressions of His people. This verse presents the central problem dealt with in this entire section. How can the terrible denunciation of sin in so many parts of the prophetic books, and even in the verses immediately before and after the present verse, be reconciled with such a promise? How can a just God, who loves holiness, forget sin? Some factor must intervene to make this possible. This factor is to be the climax of our present section of Isaiah. God intends to blot out transgression for His own sake. Yet He also intends to maintain His unsullied holiness. The importance of this problem is stressed more and more as we go through these chapters. God's solution will be revealed in the great climactic prediction in chapter 53, toward which all of this section is leading.

After the great declaration, in verse 25, of God's ultimate intention, He again points to His great sorrow over sin. He calls on His people to show any proper cause of complaint against Him. The implied answer, of course, is that man has nothing truly to declare against God. All our excuses for not doing God's will are flimsy and will not bear examination. God calls on us to try to express them clearly and thus to see how unreasonable they are.

In verse 27 He pronounces strong condemnation of the sin of Israel: "Your first father sinned, and your representatives have transgressed against me." Every part of the nation is implicated in its terrible sin.

Verse 28 declares the inevitable results. Like every calamity that can come into the life of one professing to be a follower of God, the Exile is no accident. It is God who gives Jacob to the curse.

Such statements of strong denunciation occur comparatively seldom in this section of Isaiah. They are always introduced with declarations of His great love, and usually, as in this case, they are immediately followed by passages telling of His intention to bring great blessing to His people.

# 13

## Isaiah 44-47

THUS FAR THIS SECTION has consisted of fairly short sentences with frequent and rapid transitions from one theme to another. This characteristic continues to the end of chapter 46. One exception is 44:24-28, where a string of statements is made up of participial clauses, gathering together several strands and reaching a climax in a new revelation of a specific event that the LORD will bring about. (This passage has already been discussed at some length in chapter 3 and that discussion will not be repeated here.)

We will not look in detail at all the material in chapters 44-46, which continues the characteristics that have been carefully examined in the previous chapters and repeats many of the same themes, but will content ourselves with noting new elements that emerge and discussing in more detail the verses that introduce unusual ideas or involve particular difficulties of interpretation.

Except for two phrases (46:8, 12), chapters 44-47 contain no rebuke for Israel. Nothing in them can be compared to the passages at the end of chapters 42 and 43, in which Israel's sin is strongly rebuked.

As in chapter 43, chapter 44 begins with a beautiful picture of future blessing (vv. 1-5), in which much figurative language is used.

> (1) But now hear, O Jacob my servant, and Israel, whom I have chosen. (2) Thus says the LORD who made you and formed you from the womb, who will help you. Do not fear, O Jacob, my servant, Jeshurun whom I have chosen, (3) for I will pour out water on the thirsty land and streams on the

dry ground. I will pour out my Spirit on your descendants and my blessing on your offspring, (4) and they shall spring up among the grass like willows by streams of water. (5) One will say, I am the LORD's, and another will call himself by the name of Jacob, and another will write on his hand, Belonging to the LORD, and will surname himself by the name of Israel.

As so many times before, assurance of blessing is followed by declaration of God's power, in this case stressing His eternity and the fact that He is the only God.

(6) Thus says the LORD, the King of Israel and his redeemer, the LORD of hosts: I am the first and I am the last, and apart from me there is no God. (7) Who is like me; let him proclaim and declare it. Let him lay it out in order for me since I appointed the ancient people. Let them declare the things that are coming and the events that are ahead.

Again opponents are challenged to give evidence against God's claims. The LORD's ability to predict the future is implied by the declaration that no false god can tell what is ahead.

(8) Do not fear or be afraid. Have I not long since proclaimed it to you and declared it? And you are my witnesses. Is there any God apart from me, or is there any other Rock? I know of none.

Once more the thought is stressed that the Israelites need not fear, as they are God's witnesses. It is their duty to declare that He is the only God.

This declaration is immediately followed by the longest condemnation of idolatry to be found anywhere in this section.

(9) All those who make a graven image are nothing. The things they delight in give them no advantage. Their own witnesses can neither see nor know, so they will be put to shame. (10) Who has fashioned a god or cast an idol, that is profitable for nothing? (11) See, all his associates will be put to shame; his craftsmen are only men. Let them all be gathered together, let them stand up, let them tremble, for they will be put to shame together. (12) The smith shapes iron and works it over the coals, fashioning it with hammers and work-

ing it with the strength of his arms. He becomes hungry and his strength fails. When he drinks no water he becomes faint. (13) An artisan shapes wood; he marks it with a line; he fits it with planes and delimits it with a compass, making it like the form of a man, like the beauty of mankind, to dwell in a house. (14) He cuts down cedars, or takes a cypress or an oak and lets it grow strong among the trees of the forest. He plants a fir, and the rain makes it grow. (15) Then it becomes fuel for a man. He takes a part of it and warms himself. He kindles a fire to bake bread. He also makes a god and worships it. He makes it into a carved image and falls down before it. (16) Half of it he burns in the fire. This half enables him to eat meat as he roasts it, and satisfies his hunger; he also warms himself and says, I am warm and I have seen fire. (17) But the rest of it he makes into a god for his graven image. He bows down before it and worships; he prays to it and says, Deliver me, for you are my god. (18) They do not know or understand. He has shut their eyes so that they cannot see, and their hearts so they cannot understand. (19) And no one considers, or has knowledge or understanding to say, I have burned half of it in the fire and also have baked bread over its coals. I roast meat and eat it; then I make the rest of it into an abomination; I fall down before a block of wood! (20) He feeds on ashes; a deceived heart has turned him aside, so that he cannot deliver himself or say, Is there not a lie in my right hand?

These verses repeat with more detail the criticisms of idolatry expressed in earlier passages, laying particular emphasis on the absurdity of using part of a tree for fuel and another part of the same tree to make a god to be worshiped.

After this long discussion of idolatry, two verses predict great blessing for Israel, which is here twice designated as God's Servant.

(21) Remember these things, O Jacob and Israel, for you are my servant. I have formed you; you are my servant, O Israel, you will not be forgotten by me. (22) I have blotted out your transgressions like a cloud, and your sins like mist. Return to me, for I have redeemed you. (23) Sing, O heavens, for the

LORD has done it! Shout for joy, lower parts of the earth. Break out into singing, you mountains, you forests, and every tree in it. For the LORD has redeemed Jacob and he will be glorified in Israel. (24*a*) Thus says the LORD, your redeemer, and the one who formed you from the womb:

Verse 22 must be taken as a prophetic perfect, pointing, as does 43:25, to the future fulfillment of God's plan to blot out the transgressions of His people, but adding a plea to return to Him in view of His promised salvation. Such a verse seems at first to contradict the many statements that condemn sin so strongly and stress its terrible effects; it raises the question how God can fulfill this promise and still be just and holy. Full understanding of the answer is not reached until Isaiah 53. This wonderful promise calls forth a beautiful doxology in verse 23.

The first part of verse 24, while stressing God's redemptive love, introduces the great declaration of verses 24*b*-28 that has been translated and discussed in the chapter on the king of Persia.* Such a long sentence rarely occurs in Isaiah. It all leads up to the climactic statement that Cyrus is God's instrument to cause Jerusalem to be rebuilt.

The first four verses of chapter 45, which continue the predictions about Cyrus, have already been translated and discussed in chapter 3. Verses 5-7 again stress the unique existence and almighty power of the LORD.

(5) I am the LORD, and there is no other; besides me there is no God. I will gird you though you have not known me, (6) that men may know from the rising of the sun and from the west that there is no one besides me; I am the LORD, and there is no other. (7) I form the light and create darkness. I make peace and create calamity. I am the one who does all these things.[21] (8) Shower, O heavens, from above, and let the clouds pour down righteousness; let the earth open up and salvation bear fruit, and let it cause righteousness to spring up with it. I the LORD have created it.

Although verse 5 briefly refers to Cyrus, its main idea is the fact that the LORD is the only God. Verses 6 and 7 continue to

*See pp. 25-28.

emphasize the greatness of God. Verse 8 contains another of Isaiah's beautiful doxologies.

The next verses call attention to the sovereignty of God. The all-wise Creator has a beneficent purpose in all that He does.

(9) Woe to the one who strives with his maker, like an earthen vessel among the vessels of the earth. Will the clay say to the potter, What are you doing? Will the thing you are making say, He has no hands? (10) Woe to him who says to a father, What are you begetting? Or to a woman, To what are you giving birth?

Nothing that God has created has a right to question the designs of the mighty God who sees the end from the beginning. Yet in the next verse the LORD graciously invites His people to inquire about His purposes.

(11) Thus says the LORD, the Holy One of Israel, and its maker: Ask me about the things to come concerning my sons, and you may command me concerning the work of my hands.

God condescends to allow His creatures to understand some of His purposes. The next few verses stress His power and His determination to free His people.

(12) I have made the earth and created man upon it. My hands have stretched out the heavens, and I have commanded all their host. (13) I have raised him up in righteousness, and I will direct all his ways. He shall build my city, and he shall let go my captives, not for price or reward, says the LORD of hosts. (14) Thus says the LORD, The work of Egypt and the merchandise of Ethiopia and of the Sabeans, men of stature, will come over unto you, and they will be yours. They will follow you. They will come over in chains and fall down before you and will make supplication to you saying, Truly God is in you and there is no other, there is no other God. (15) Surely you are a God who hides himself, O God of Israel, the Saviour.

Although man has no inherent right to know the future and can find true happiness only in putting complete trust in the

God who is perfect in wisdom and love, the LORD chooses, in this case, to give renewed assurance about His plan to deliver His people. He declares that He, who has created all things (v. 12), is bringing Cyrus to accomplish His righteous purposes. Cyrus will be God's instrument to cause that Jerusalem be rebuilt and to permit the exiles to go free (v. 13).

As so often in the prophetic revelation, the vision of the prophet focuses on near events and then looks further and gives a glimpse of events in the more distant future. The first half of verse 14 seems to be a prediction that Egypt, Ethiopia, and Sheba will come into Cyrus's hands (as in 43:3).† This prediction was fulfilled when these lands were conquered by Cyrus's son, Cambyses. As the verse continues, it includes predictions that, so far as we know, were not fulfilled at that time. Most commentators take Egypt, Ethiopia, and Sheba here as representing the various nations of mankind and pointing to an ultimate conversion of these nations to the true God. Acts 8:27-39 tells of an Ethiopian court official who received the message of salvation and carried it back to his country. In the early years of the Christian era thriving churches were established in these regions. Later that area was to a large extent overrun by the Muslims, and much of it has remained in Islamic hands for more than a thousand years. It is hard to know whether the latter part of this verse is a prediction of those few centuries of Christian dominance in these areas or whether it points to something still future.

It seems most reasonable to consider verse 15 as part of the statement by the new converts as they marvel at their previous inability to recognize the true God and now see that He is indeed the Holy One of Israel, the Saviour.

Many interpreters differ with this interpretation of verse 15, thinking instead that it expresses Isaiah's own wonder as God's great plan unfolds (cf. Rom 11:33).

> (16) They shall be put to shame and confounded, all of them;
> the makers of idols shall go to confusion together. (17) But
> Israel has been saved by the LORD with an everlasting salva-

†Cf. pp. 79-80.

tion. You will not be put to shame or humiliated to all eternity. (18) For thus says the LORD, who created the heavens. He is the God who formed the earth and made it; he established it and did not create it to be a waste place, but formed it to be inhabited: I am the LORD and there is no other. (19) I have not spoken in secret, in some dark land. I did not say to the offspring of Jacob, Seek me in a waste place. I the LORD speak righteousness, declaring things that are right.[22]

Again the folly of idol worship is contrasted with God's mercy to Israel, and this is followed by renewed emphasis on His righteous plans.

The next verses again challenge the idolaters and declare that the LORD is the only God.

(20) Assemble yourselves and come. Draw near together, you that escaped of the nations. They have no knowledge who carry about their wooden idol, who pray to a god that cannot save. (21) Declare and present your case; let them consult together. Who has announced this from of old? Who has long since declared it? Have not I, the LORD? There is no other god besides me, a righteous God and a Saviour; there is none except me.

The final verses of chapter 45 declare God's saving purpose for all the ends of the earth, and His determination universally to establish His righteousness. Verse 25 again places emphasis on His beneficent purpose for His people Israel.

(22) Turn to me and be saved, all the ends of the earth, for I am God and there is no other. (23) I have sworn by myself, the word has gone forth from my mouth in righteousness and will not return, that to me every knee shall bow, every tongue shall swear. (24) They will say of me, Only in the LORD are righteousness and strength. Men will come to him and all who were angry at him will be put to shame. (25) In the LORD all the offspring of Israel will be justified and will glory.

The first two verses of chapter 46 declare that Bel and Nabu, the two leading gods of Babylon, will be defeated and themselves will go into captivity. The rest of chapter 46 repeats the same themes as the previous chapters: God's mercy to Israel; condemnation of idolatry; emphasis on God's existence and power; and special stress on His ability to predict the future, as shown particularly by the prophecies about Cyrus.

The chapter is rather unique in that it has two brief phrases rebuking Israel (in vv. 8, 12), although the rest of its emphasis is entirely on His love and mercy.

All fifteen verses of chapter 47 are devoted to the destruction of Babylonian power and thus form a conclusion to Part 1 of this section of Isaiah. Everything has been leading up to the complete overthrow of this nation holding the Israelites in subjection. Babylon is thought of as a princess who, after ruling a great empire, is now to be reduced to the position of a servant girl. In verse 6 Babylon is particularly rebuked for having laid a very heavy yoke on God's people and shown them no mercy, even though God Himself had given Israel into Babylon's hands as a punishment for its sins. This thought is strikingly paralleled in Isaiah's discussion of the Assyrian power in Isaiah 10:5-19.

Verses 7-8 picture the pride of Babylon in its past accomplishments,[23] during more than a thousand years, and declare that all this greatness will come to a sudden end. In succeeding verses much is said about the sorceries, the enchantments, the astrologers, and the stargazers of Babylon. During the last one hundred fifty years, discovery and decipherment of the writings of ancient Babylon have shown how large a part such practices played in its activities. Hundreds of clay tables describe alleged methods of determining the future by examining the entrails of animals[24] and by other magical practices. Isaiah predicts that all of this will prove worthless.

The final verse deals with the merchants from many parts of the world who were accustomed to bring their products to Babylon. When the city loses its power they will give it no help, but will rapidly return to their homelands with no sympathy for the city from which they had formerly drawn so much of their profit.

92

Part 2

# Israel Released and the Lord's Servant Individualized

# 14

## Isaiah 48

WITH THIS CHAPTER we enter the second main part of our section of Isaiah.[25] In Part 2 most of the units of material dealing with related thoughts are longer than before. The symphonic structure, so characteristic of chapters 40 to 46, with its frequent shifts from strong expression of one emotion to equally strong expression of another, is no longer clearly in evidence, though existing in greatly modified form in chapter 48. In Part 2, reiterations of the themes of God's power, of His ability to predict the future, and of idolatry become less frequent, though all three are found in chapter 48. This chapter also contains the final reference to Cyrus.

Up to this point there has been no direct accusation of idol worship against Israel. Except for a few passages where Israel's sin was strongly condemned, the general attitude has been that on the one side there are God's people, serving Him and looking to Him for help, but sometimes tending to give way to despair because they see no evidence that help is coming; while on the other side there are the heathen, whom God condemns for worshiping idols. The Israelites are constantly reminded that these idols are powerless and cannot predict the future. At the beginning of chapter 46 it was declared that the great Mesopotamian gods were themselves to go into captivity, and all of chapter 47 describes the downfall of Babylon.

In Part 1 there were comparatively few passages in which Israel was rebuked for its sin, and most of these were presented as explanations of the reason the nation had gone into exile. With chapter 48 there is a marked change of emphasis. In this chapter the Israelites themselves are directly accused of idolatry, and their sin is emphasized far more than in any previous chapter of our section.

Except for two brief phrases in chapter 46, every verse in Part 1 in which Israel was rebuked for sin was clearly separated from the verses in which deliverance was promised. The transition from one thought to the other was sudden and complete.

In chapter 48, the two emphases are sometimes joined in the same verse. In this chapter, two contrasted thoughts are intertwined: (1) God will deliver His people; and (2) the people are unworthy of deliverance.

> (1) Hear this, O house of Jacob, who are named Israel and who came forth from the loins of Judah, who swear by the name of the LORD and invoke the God of Israel, but not in truth nor in righteousness. (2) For they call themselves of the holy city, and lean on the God of Israel—the LORD of hosts is his name.

Nearly all of this passage sounds like an assurance that Israel is God's people, who swears by His name, leans upon Him, and will receive His blessing. Yet the last few words of the first verse change the whole effect, for these words declare that when the Israelites invoke the name of God, they do so neither in truth nor in righteousness.

This is the strongest direct rebuke of Israel that has occurred thus far in this section of Isaiah. There was nothing quite comparable to it in chapters 40-47. The contrast between the end of verse 1 and the rest of verses 1-2 is very sharp. Yet these words have been accurately preserved through centuries of copying and recopying of manuscripts. This fact provides remarkable evidence of the fidelity of the Hebrew scribes who copied exactly what they found in their manuscripts, even when it included such strong criticism of their own people.

Never before in our section have the Israelites been called hypocrites. In previous passages of rebuke, they have been criticized for past disobedience to God, which made it necessary for Him to send them into exile. Here they are accused of present and continuing sin, and are pictured as loudly proclaiming their loyalty to God but not doing so in truth or in righteousness.

As the message continues, the accusation is even stronger:

> (3) I declared the former things from the beginning. They went forth from my mouth and I caused you to hear them. I made them occur suddenly (4) because I know that you are obstinate; your neck is an iron sinew and your forehead bronze. (5) I declared them to you long ago; before they occurred I announced them to you, lest you should say, My idol did them, my carved image and my molten image ordered them.

The LORD declares that He told them what He would do long before it happened because He knew that otherwise His people would give an idol credit for their deliverance instead of attributing it to God.

The accusation in these verses has much relevance to modern times, when men so commonly make an idol of human ability and achievement. This may be illustrated by the escape of the British soldiers from Dunkirk.

When the Belgian army surrendered to Hitler in 1940 the Germans closed in on the British forces in France, driving them toward the port of Dunkirk. With the English Channel in front and German troops on every other side, it appeared certain that within a few days all of the British soldiers would be captured or killed. In England thousands of people thronged the churches, praying that God would give deliverance. Then a strange thing occurred. For several days the English Channel, usually so rough that it was dangerous for small vessels to cross, was remarkably calm. Everyone who had even a small boat rushed across the Channel to rescue some of the soldiers. During this time the sky was heavily overcast with clouds. Since radar was not yet available to the German planes and they were unable to see through the clouds and fog to learn the location of the troops or of the rescue ships, they could not effectively bomb the British troops that were crowding onto the piers. Many thousands were rescued, and a great paean of praise to God for His deliverance went up throughout the British Isles.

97

Before long, however, all this was forgotten and the deliverance was attributed to the bravery of the Royal Air Force and the diligence of the rescuers.

Today's idol is humanity. Man is proud of his great exploits. In common use and in legal terminology, the phrase *an act of God* has come to be used, not to point to signs of God's wonderful goodness, but almost exclusively as meaning a catastrophe.

(6) You have heard: now see all this! Will you not declare it? Now I proclaim new things to you, hidden things that you have not known. (7) They are created now, not long ago. Before today you had not heard of them, lest you should say, See, I knew them.

The same criticism of human refusal to recognize God's goodness and power, just as applicable today as ever, is repeated. It leads to a short but emphatic rebuke.

(8) Indeed you have not heard, indeed you have not known. From long ago your ear has not been opened. For I knew that you would deal very treacherously; you have been called a rebel from birth.

Yet this rebuke is followed by promises of renewed mercy.

(9) For the sake of my name I will delay my wrath. For my praise I restrain it from you, so as not to cut you off. (10) See, I have refined you, but not as silver. I have tested you in the furnace of affliction (11) for my own sake. For my own sake I will act. For how should my name be profaned? I will not give my glory to another.

In these verses the LORD declares that in spite of Israel's faithlessness He is going to defer His anger in order to accomplish His own purposes. He is preparing and testing them in order to accomplish His plan. Despite the weakness and sinfulness of humanity, He will not allow His name to be permanently profaned.

(12) Listen to me, O Jacob and Israel whom I called. I am

he, I am the first, I am also the last. (13) Surely my hand founded the earth, and my right hand spread out the heavens. When I call to them they stand together.

These two verses again emphasize God's eternity and His power over nature.

(14) Assemble all of you and listen. Who among them has declared these things? The LORD has loved him. He shall carry out his good pleasure on Babylon, and his arm shall be against the Chaldeans. (15) I, even I, have spoken; indeed I have called him, I have brought him, and he will make his way successful.

This is the final declaration that God will send Cyrus to overwhelm the Chaldeans. It has already been discussed in detail.*

This prediction of the coming of Cyrus is followed by a remarkable verse that can hardly be understood without looking ahead to chapter 49.

(16) Come near to me, hear this. From the beginning I have not spoken in secret. From the time it came to be,[26] I was there. And now the Lord GOD has sent me, and his Spirit.

Sometimes it is difficult to know whether the prophet is speaking in his own person, whether he speaks as representing his nation, or whether he is presenting the words that God speaks. Thus in 42:24 the prophet seems to speak as representing the nation. The first two verses of chapter 48 could well represent the prophet as speaking, since he speaks of God in the third person. The beginning of the next verse could easily be thought of as representing the prophet pointing back to his former messages, but the last part of the verse shows clearly that the LORD, rather than the prophet, is speaking, since it says, "I made them occur." Similarly, the use of the first person pronoun in 48:12-13, 15 indicates that the LORD Himself is speaking. In verse 15, the fact that the speaker declares that He Himself has given Cyrus power to overcome the Chaldeans makes it obvious that the LORD is the one who is speaking. The

*See pp. 25-30.

same is true in verse 17 where the LORD again speaks in the first person.

In the case of verse 16 an interesting problem appears. These can hardly be the prophet's own words, for he says: "From the beginning I have not spoken in secret. From the time it came to be I am there." Yet the final line of the verse says, "And now the Lord GOD has sent me, and his Spirit." Here the speaker says that the LORD has sent him. The prophet can hardly be the speaker, since he has just used terms that could apply only to the eternal God. Yet it appears very strange to think that the LORD is speaking, since the speaker declares that the Lord GOD has sent him.

For the answer to the problem, it is necessary to look ahead a few verses, to the beginning of chapter 49. In 49:1-5 the speaker is obviously the Servant of the LORD. This is quite evident in verses 1-4 and becomes unmistakable in verse 5, which reads in part: "And now says the LORD, who formed me from the womb to be his servant." It is therefore not at all unreasonable to consider the possibility that the Servant of the LORD is already speaking in 48:16. When He says, "From the beginning I have not spoken in secret," one may think of the theophanies of the Old Testament and of the many revelations that were given to various prophets. "From the time it came to be I was there" suggests His preexistence and His eternity. Yet the words, "the Lord GOD has sent me," definitely imply a distinction in the Godhead. He is the LORD, and yet the LORD sends Him. The Eternal One has been sent by the Lord GOD and His Spirit. Thus the doctrine of the Trinity finds perhaps its clearest Old Testament expression in this verse.

The words "and his Spirit" occupy an ambiguous position in the Hebrew sentence and can equally well be considered part of the subject or part of the object. God the Father has sent the Son and has sent the Spirit. God the Father and the Spirit have sent the Son. Some translations take the words "his Spirit" as part of the subject, some as part of the object. The Hebrew can be read either way; both are true.

In 48:14-16, the two great emphases of this section of Isaiah are brought into close juxtaposition. Verses 14-15 describe Cyrus as the one whom God will use to accomplish His purpose of freeing the Israelites from bondage. Verse 16 presents the One who is to perform an even greater deliverance.

(17) Thus says the LORD, your Redeemer, the Holy One of Israel; I am the LORD your God who teaches you to profit, who leads you in the way you should go. (18)O that you had listened to my commandments; then your peace would have been like a river and your righteousness like the waves of the sea. (19) Your offspring would have been like the sand and your descendants like its grains. Their name would never be cut off or destroyed from before me.

Again God expresses His great disappointment that Israel has not kept His commandments, and He reminds them of the great blessings that could have been theirs if they had followed His desires. Yet this expression of disappointment is immediately followed by a very strong assurance that God will deliver them from the Babylonian Captivity, followed by a reminder of the way God blessed His people as they made the long trip from Egypt to Palestine.

(20) Depart from Babylon! Flee from the Chaldeans! Declare with a voice of singing. Tell this, utter it even to the end of the earth; say, the LORD has redeemed his servant Jacob. (21) And they did not thirst when he led them through the desert. He caused the water to flow out of the rock for them. He split the rock, and the waters gushed out.

The reminder of the way God provided for His people when they came out of Egypt serves as a suggestion that similar blessings will be theirs as they start the much longer trip from Babylon to the land of Israel.

(22) There is no peace, says the LORD, for the wicked.

Verse 22 might seem rather incongruous in such proximity to the great promises of blessing that immediately precede; but actually it fits right into the pattern, which has been followed throughout the chapter, of combining promises of great bless-

**101**

ing to God's people with statements of His wrath against their wickedness.

How can God glorify Himself through individuals who have so turned away from Him? This question keeps recurring and is constantly presented to the mind, even if not expressed verbally. By the many sharp contrasts, the impression is being created that something very serious must be done about the sin question. Otherwise deliverance will eventually be followed by another exile, as sin continues to assert itself among the people.

# 15

## The Individualization of the Servant of the Lord: Isaiah 49:1-12

WE NOW COME to the second extensive passage on this vital theme. Its first seven verses read as follows:

> (1) Listen to me, coastlands, and pay attention, people from afar. The LORD called me from the womb; from the body of my mother he caused my name to be remembered. (2) And he made my mouth like a sharp sword; in the shadow of his hand he hid me, he made me a polished arrow, in his quiver he hid me. (3) And he said to me, You are my servant, Israel, in whom I will be glorified. (4) But I said, I have toiled in vain; I have spent my strength for nothing and uselessly; yet surely my judgment is with the LORD, and my work with my God.[27] (5) And now says the LORD who formed me from the womb to be his servant, to bring Jacob back to him, in order that Israel might be gathered to him, for I am honored in the eyes of the LORD, and my God is my strength. (6) And he said, It is too small a thing that you should be my servant to raise up the tribes of Jacob, and to restore those preserved of Israel; I will also make you a light to the nations, so that my salvation may reach to the end of the earth. (7) Thus says the LORD, the Redeemer of Israel, and its Holy One, to the despised one, to the one abhorred by the nation, to the servant of rulers: kings shall see and rise, princes shall prostrate themselves, because of the LORD who is faithful, the Holy One of Israel who has chosen you.

This passage was doubtless included among those that Jesus explained to the disciples after His resurrection (Luke 24:27). It contains many thoughts that would previously have been difficult for the disciples to understand. Readers in Isaiah's day may have been puzzled by some of its statements, but certain thoughts stand out very clearly in it. (1) It has much in common with 42:1-7, since it too declares that the Servant of the LORD is to be a light to the Gentiles. (2) Verse 3 says, "You are my Servant Israel," thus still equating the Servant with Israel in some respects, though, as we have seen, the term could not possibly designate the entire nation. (3) Although the Servant is called Israel, He is here clearly differentiated from Israel, since verses 5-6 say that He is to bring Jacob back to God, to raise up the tribes of Jacob, and to restore those preserved of Israel. Thus this passage makes it clear that the Servant is an individual, apart from Israel, even though He is to fulfill Israel's responsibility.

In these seven verses it is obvious that the Servant Himself is the speaker, though a great part of what He says consists of telling what the LORD has said to Him.

The first two verses have a tone very similar to 42:1-7. The attention of the distant lands is called to the fact that the speaker has been set apart for a very special task and has been given divine preparation and divine protection. The last part of the first verse was fulfilled when the angel told Mary, long before the birth of her Son, that she should call His name Jesus (Luke 1:31), and later gave the same command to Joseph (Matt 1: 21).

Verse 2 begins, "And he made my mouth like a sharp sword." This points to the inexhaustible teachings of Christ, who spoke with authority and not like the scribes (Matt 7:29; Mark 1: 22). Paul said that when the Lord returns He will smite the wicked one "with the spirit of his mouth" (2 Thess 2:8). John saw Him in glory with a sharp sword proceeding out of His mouth (Rev 1:16; 19:15, 21).

The second and fourth clauses of verse 2 describe the divine protection of the Servant. Its third clause, "he made me like a polished arrow," points to His special preparation for His work and to the fact that like a polished arrow He will speed unerringly to the goal for which He came into the world.

Verse 3 identified the Servant with Israel, and indeed **He** **must** come from Israel, so that He can represent Israel in doing **the** work for which Israel has responsibility. As we have no- ticed, later verses show that He is to do a work for Israel as **well** as for the nations, thereby indicating that He is an **individual** who can be distinguished from the Israelite nation.

At the end of verse 3 the LORD declares that His glorious purposes will be established through the work of His **Servant.** This reminds us of John 1:14, "And the Word was made **flesh,** and dwelt among us (and we beheld his glory, the glory as **of** the only begotten of the Father,) full of grace and truth."

Thus far the tone of absolute confidence and certainty of **ac-** complishing the work is identical with that in 42:1-7. **Verse** 4 seems to strike a discordant note: "But I said, I have toiled **in** vain; I have spent my strength for nothing and uselessly; yet surely my judgment is with the LORD, and my work with **my** God." It may seem hard to think of such words being said **by** one whose absolute confidence and unwavering forward prog- ress could be described as it was in 42:1-7.

In view of the earlier passages in which we have seen the in- ability of Israel to perform the work described, we must con- sider the possibility that in verse 4 the nation as a whole is speaking, thinking of its responsibility and feeling its inade- quacy. However, a little reflection shows that this interpreta- tion is not correct. The reason for Israel's inability to perform the work is not that it has toiled in vain, but that its sin and un- faithfulness have resulted in spiritual blindness and have made it necessary that God send it into exile.

Obviously, then, some other interpretation must be found. It must point, instead, to a time of discouragement in the course of the work of the Servant. The New Testament shows **that** there was indeed such a period during our Lord's earthly **min-** istry. The crowds began to thin out, and the faithful **disciples** seemed unable to grasp the true intent of His messages. **The** time came when He even said to the twelve, "Will ye also **go** away?" (John 6:67). Chapter 42 and most of chapter 49 **em-** phasize His exaltation and the success of His work. **This verse**

**105**

is the first suggestion of another phase of His experience—His humiliation and apparent failure.

The last part of the verse is sometimes translated, "the justice due me is with the LORD, and my recompense [or reward] is with my God." Objection to this rendering must be made on two counts, as follows:

1. While the insertion "due me" is possible, it is probably not correct. The Hebrew word rendered "my judgment" may refer to one's activity in establishing justice or to his receiving the justice due him. It is unlikely that the latter is what the Servant has in mind. It is far more probable that He is saying that though visible results of His work appear at this point to be lacking, He knows that the Lord will use Him to perform the assigned task.

2. The translation "my recompense [or reward]" has little warrant. The word that we have translated "my work" is a noun related to the common verb pā'al, meaning "do" or "act." This noun occurs in a number of contexts where "toil," "labor," or "activity" is clearly meant. Only in one case does the meaning "wages" seem desirable (Lev 19: 13), and even there it may be a term to indicate the results of labor. While there are several other Hebrew words that have the definite meaning of "reward" or "wages," evidence of such a meaning for this word is almost entirely lacking. Our Lord is not here thinking of receiving a reward but of accomplishing the work for which He came into the world.

Verse 5 again refers to the fact that the LORD "formed me from the womb," and may possibly refer to the virgin birth. It continues with the statement that the bringing back of Israel is included in the Servant's work, a fact that readers of chapter 42 might not have expected, since the emphasis in that chapter is almost entirely on His worldwide ministry.

We have translated part of this verse, "in order that Israel might be gathered to him." The King James Version renders it, "though Israel be not gathered." The two translations represent a variant reading preserved in the Hebrew manuscripts, which involves a difference of only one letter.[28] Actually, decision between the two does not affect the meaning of the passage, since the previous clause already states one of these meanings, and the interpretation in the King James Version is merely an anticipation of what will be clearly said in verse 6. (An identical textual variation in Isaiah 9:3 results in a similar difference between translations.)

Verse 6 begins with a hyperbole. The raising up of the tribes of Jacob is not a small thing but a great task. Calling it a small thing is simply a rhetorical way of indicating that the Servant has also a far greater task to perform, that of bringing light to the nations and salvation to the ends of the earth.

Verse 7 has the first clear statement of the humiliation of the Servant, a thought briefly suggested in verse 4. When the verse speaks of Him as "the one abhorred by the nation," it would seem definitely to point to the rejection of Christ by a large portion of the nation of Israel. The latter part of the verse strongly emphasizes His exaltation, which will result in the submission of great kings and princes.

Throughout this passage, the faithfulness of God is emphasized. It will be God in Christ who will bring salvation to the world (2 Cor 5:19).

There are five more verses in this passage, which read as follows:

> (8) Thus says the LORD, In a favorable time I have answered you, and in a day of salvation I have helped you; and I will protect you and give you for a covenant of a people, to restore the land, and to make them inherit the desolate heritages; (9) saying to the prisoners, Go forth, to those who are in darkness, Show yourselves. They will feed along the roads, and their pasture will be on all their heights. (10) They will not hunger or thirst, nor will scorching heat or sun strike them, for he who has compassion on them will lead them, and will guide them to springs of water. (11) And I will make all my mountains a road, and my highways will be raised up. (12) Behold, these will come from the north and from the west, and these from the land of Sinim.

These verses deal particularly with the outworking of the activity of the Servant. As we examine them, we should have in mind the great emphases that have stood out in our section thus far. We have seen that much attention has been given to the release of the exiles from captivity, even to naming the human instrument God would use to make it possible that those who desired should be able to return to their homeland. We have also seen that there is a gradually increasing realization that the problem of sin must be handled, or this return from exile will be only a temporary help. There has also been introduced the great figure of the Servant of the LORD, who is to bring light to the nations and to establish justice in all the earth.

It would be natural for an exile to find great comfort in these verses. The Servant is to be a covenant of the people; He will restore the land (v. 8). He will enable the true heirs again to possess the desolate inheritances—a natural term for the divisions into which Joshua had apportioned the land. These possessions were passed on from father to son through many generations, but as a result of the Exile they became utterly desolate.

Israel has been described as a prisoner, one who is blind, one who must make a long and difficult trip if he is to get back to his own land. There are many statements in these verses that would apply to these needs. The passage promises that prisoners will be released and that there will be provision for food and comfort on the long journey (v. 9). Water will be plentiful (v. 10), and the natural barriers will not interfere (v. 11). All this would bring great comfort to those whose eyes were focused on the desired release from exile.

Yet, in light of the context, another idea seems to be meant. Since our present passage deals with the great work of the Servant of the LORD, and since we have noticed in it many verses thus far that cannot be interpreted in any reasonable way except in relation to the coming of the promised Redeemer, it is reasonable to conclude that the latter is the primary emphasis in these five verses also. Besides, parts of verse 8 seem to look beyond the Babylonian Exile. This is particularly true of verse 12, as well, since it speaks of those who will come from far more distant points and from other directions. In the Babylonian Exile the prisoners were transported to the east, not to the north or to the west.

Verse 8 begins with a reference to a specific time when God will provide salvation. Paul quotes this verse in 2 Corinthians 6:2. The same apostle says, "When the fulness of the time was come, God sent forth his Son" (Gal 4:4). Jesus told the disciples that the time of His return was kept in the Father's hands and not to be known by them (Acts 1:7). Although there are many occasions when we do not know God's timing, we can be sure that it is exactly right and that He works all things together for the good of His people.

In the latter part of the verse God promises to protect the Servant and make Him the fulfillment of God's covenant promise to David. Through Him all that sin has wrecked will be restored and the desolate inheritances reestablished.

Verse 9 reiterates the promise of 42:7, that the Servant will bring out the prisoners and those who sit in darkness, and adds the promise of nourishment along the way.

Verse 10 can be understood as a beautiful statement in figurative terms of the spiritual blessings that God will give His people.

Verse 11 promises that the great obstacles that seem so formidable will be turned into roads for the progress of those who belong to the Redeemer.

Verse 12 describes the outreach of the work of the Servant of the Lord. The salvation that He provides is not to be limited to a small group. The fact that His work is to reach people of distant lands was stressed in chapter 42 and repeated to some extent in the earlier verses of chapter 49. Verse 12 pictures the people as coming from far off. It names two specific directions, the north and the west. The Babylonian army had come from the east and had taken its prisoners into captivity in that direction. A few had fled to the south, into Egypt. There is no evidence that any of the people were transported either to the north or to the west during the Babylonian Exile. This verse pictures the redeemed coming from far away, some from the north and some from the west and some "from the land of Sinim."

From time to time various interpretations have been suggested for the phrase "the land of Sinim." The Hebrew plural ending (*-im*) is often included in its name for a nation. Many commentators, particularly before the rise of the modern critical theories, were quite convinced that the word referred to the land of China. Even today, experts in the study of Chinese are called "Sinologists."

Scholars differ as to the origin of the term by which China is known in the West. Some suggest that our word *China* may have come originally from the name of one of its western sections, called Ch'in (or Ts'in), which might have been the part first entered by traders going to China. It would have been quite natural for them to designate the whole area after its nearest part, just as Europeans have come to designate the whole continent of Asia by the name of the Roman province they entered first, which we now call Asia Minor.

Archaeological evidence is available to show that products of China were being transported into the Near East well before the time of Isaiah.

In the providence of God, the ruler of the region called Ch'in (or Ts'in) was able to conquer the rest of China in 221 B.C. and to establish a unified control, taking to himself the name "First Emperor." He centralized the administration of the empire, dividing it into thirty-six provinces, and built more than half of the Great Wall of China. This emperor left a great impression on the future development of the country, although his dynasty lasted only a short time. It has been suggested that the name foreigners use for China, different from that by which its own people designate their area, originated as a result of this ruler's achievements. It is most interesting that God led the prophet thus to use the name that would eventually come to represent all China as an indication of the wide outreach of the work of the LORD's Servant.

Today strong atheistic forces hold the Chinese mainland in subjection and prohibit the preaching of the Gospel. We may well take heart from Isaiah's prophecy in verse 12 and hope that there may yet be another great period of Gospel preaching in that land, if our Lord tarries.

The present tendency among critical scholars is to insist that "Sinim" must be a reference to Syene, a small town at the extreme southern end of Egypt. They point out that in Ezekiel 29:10 and 30:6 the words "from Migdol to Syene" are probably used to designate the entire land of Egypt. Since north and west are specified in the verse, they assert that this must be a reference to the south, and must therefore point to Syene (modern Aswan). The word is actually translated "Syene" in the Revised Standard Version.

There are serious objections to the view that "Sinim" means Syene. (1) It would be very unusual to add the plural ending to the name of a small town. (2) It would be strange to put the words "land of" before the name of a small town. (3) While *Syene* is a useful term to indicate the southern end of Egypt, it was a comparatively insignificant town at the time of Isaiah and, for several centuries afterward, much less important than Yeb, on the neighboring island of Elephantine. The suggestion that "Sinim" represents Syene is highly questionable.

In addition, the fact that north and west are mentioned does not necessarily mean that Sinim must be in the south. A reference to the east would be equally possible, and in fact more probable. Mention of north and west, directions to which no exiles had been taken, shows that the phrase looks far beyond Babylonian Exile; but it would be quite natural to include a reference to an eastern point, showing that God's mercy would eventually reach even to the distant land of China, far beyond Babylon.[29]

After these twelve verses, with their breathtaking presentation of the tremendous things to be accomplished by the Servant

111

of the LORD and the worldwide outreach of His activity, in verse 13 the prophet breaks out into another doxology similar to the one in 44:23.

> (13) Sing for joy, O heavens, and rejoice, O earth! Break forth into singing, O mountains! For the LORD has comforted his people, and will have compassion on his afflicted.

# 16

## God Answers Israel's Cry of Despair: Isaiah 49:14—50:3

DESPITE THE WONDERFUL PROMISES in 49:1-12, followed by the beautiful doxology in verse 13, Israel may be imagined as thinking, *These are wonderful pictures of marvelous acts that God may perform in the distant future, but what good will this do me, enduring suffering and humiliation with no hope of deliverance?* In verse 14 she utters a cry of despair:

> But Zion said, The LORD has forsaken me; my Lord has forgotten me.

It is characteristic of humanity to have periods of doubt about God's great goodness. Here the Lord speaks to Isaiah's godly followers. These believing Israelites, knowing that the sin of their nation was so great that exile must inevitably come, might tend to give way to despair and even decide that there was no future for their nation or for their religion.

God answers Zion's despondent words with three arguments, each expressed in the form of a question.

1.  "Can a woman forget her sucking child, that she should not have compassion on the son of her womb?" (49:15).
2.  "Can prey be taken from the mighty, or the captives of a tyrant be rescued?" (49:24).
3.  "Thus says the LORD, where is the certificate of divorce by which I have sent your mother away?" (50:1).

Each of these questions is followed by an explanation.

113

1. The love of God to His people is far greater than the natural love of a woman for her child.
2. The brutal tyrant may be far stronger than his victim, but God is still stronger and will overcome the tyrant.
3. There is no basis for thinking that God has forsaken Israel. He is punishing her for her transgressions, but His relationship with her, which is compared to that of a husband to a wife, will never be broken, and His power will be exerted for her deliverance.

In addition to the three answers, the LORD gives a beautiful glimpse of blessings that He promises to send in the more distant future (vv. 17-23). This passage is presented immediately after the first of the three answers, which reads as follows:

> (14) But Zion said, The LORD has forsaken me, and my Lord has forgotten me. (15) Can a woman forget her nursing child that she should not have compassion on the son of her womb? Even these may forget, but I will not forget you. (16) See, I have inscribed you on the palms of my hands. Your walls are continually before me.

In this first of the three answers, God declares that His love is far greater than any human love. The next verses look far into the future.

> (17) Your builders hurry; your destroyers and devastators will depart from you. (18) Lift up your eyes and look around. All of them gather themselves together, they come to you. As I live, declares the LORD, you will surely put all of them on as jewels and bind them on as a bride. (19) For your waste and desolate places and your destroyed land will now become too narrow for the inhabitants, and those who swallowed you will be far away. (20) The children of your bereavement will yet say in your ears, The place is too narrow for me; make room for me to dwell in. (21) Then you will say in your heart, Who has begotten these for me, seeing I have lost my children and am barren, an exile and a wanderer? Who has reared these? See, I was left alone. Where did these come from? (22) Thus says the Lord GOD, See, I will lift up my hand to

the nations and set my standard to the peoples, and they will bring your sons in their arms and your daughters will be carried on their shoulders. (23) And kings will be your guardians, and their queens your nursing mothers. They will bow down to you with their faces to the earth, and lick the dust of your feet, and you will know that I am the LORD. Those who hopefully wait for me will not be put to shame.

Even though the center of attention moved back, in verses 14-16, to the time of the Exile, much of the picture in verses 17-23 looks far beyond anything that took place at that time.

An era is described in which the children of Zion will be far more numerous than ever before. They are not necessarily natural children, for verse 21 asks the question, "Who has begotten these for me, seeing I have lost my children? . . . Who has reared these? . . . Where did these come from?" It is not at all unnatural to take this as a picture of the new branches grafted into the olive tree described in Romans 11:24, though physically derived from a different source. Such an interpretation of verse 21 would suggest that verses 22-23 look to the extension of the knowledge of the true God throughout the world.

In the first part of verse 17, the King James Version reads, "Thy children shall make haste." By a slight change of vowels, the Hebrew word here translated "children" could be translated "builders,"[30] and the word is so rendered in many modern versions. Although there can be little question that in most cases knowledge of the original vowels has been correctly preserved, there are undoubtedly some instances where a vowel was not correctly remembered during the centuries prior to the time when vowels began to be indicated by signs in the text, perhaps as late as the tenth century after Christ. The Septuagint took this word to mean "builders," and this rendering was followed by the Vulgate. Actually it makes little difference which reading is adopted here, since both are true. The passage clearly predicts that Zion will be rebuilt; it also predicts a great increase in the number of its children. In the nearer context, *builders* might seem to fit better; in view of the following verses, with their great emphasis on children, an equally cogent argument might be made that *children* is meant.

This portion ends with a general exhortation to every believer: "Those who hopefully wait for me will not be put to shame."

With verse 24 the prophet returns to the immediate situation.

> (24) Can the prey be taken from the mighty, or the captives of a tyrant be rescued? (25) But thus says the LORD, even the captives of the mighty will be taken away, and the prey of the tyrant will be rescued; for I will contend with the one who contends with you, and I will save your sons. (26) I will make your oppressors eat their own flesh, and they will become drunk with their own blood as with wine, and all flesh will know that I, the LORD, am your Saviour and your Redeemer, the mighty One of Jacob.

As the second answer to Israel's cry of despair, God again uses a rhetorical question: "Can the prey be taken from a mighty man, or the captives of a tyrant be rescued?" (v. 24). Then He says that this may indeed happen. There is no human force so great that a greater may not overcome it. But God's power is far superior to that of any human conqueror. No matter how strong the tyrant who holds God's people in subjection, God is stronger. Though He may allow wickedness to triumph for a time, He gives the promise, "I will save your children."

This verse should give great comfort to Christians living in Communist dominated lands, where meetings for prayer and worship are often brutally disrupted. Christian leaders are imprisoned and tortured, and often their children are sent to orphan homes to be raised as atheists. God says that He will contend with those who contend with His people and will save their children. In God's own time, the oppressors will be utterly destroyed.

The answer to Zion's complaint is continued in the next three verses, though the chapter division has been wrongly placed.

> (50:1) Thus says the LORD, where is the certificate of divorce by which I have sent your mother away? Or to which of my

creditors did I sell you? Behold, you were sold for your iniquities, and it was for your trangressions that your mother was sent away. (2) Why was there no man when I came? Why, when I called, was there no one to answer? Is my hand shortened so that it cannot redeem? Have I no power to deliver? Behold, at my rebuke I dry up the sea, I make rivers a wilderness, their fish stink for lack of water and die of thirst. (3) I clothe the heavens with blackness and make sackcloth their covering.

God declares that His relation to Israel is unchanged. Her sins require punishment but He will deliver her with supernatural power.

There is an unfortunate verse division between verses 2 and 3. Although the verse divisions in the Bible are much older than the chapter divisions, they were not part of the original writing. In a few places they are almost ludicrously wrong (as in Psalm 19:4-5.) Some verses consist of only a small part of a sentence. Others include two or three sentences.

Isaiah 50:3 is a continuation of the last part of verse 2 and really should be combined with it. If that would make too long a verse, the division should have been made at the end of the series of questions in verse 2. After verse 3 there is a very sharp change of thought; Isaiah 50:4 should really begin a new chapter.

# 17

## The Servant's Soliloquy: Isaiah 50:4-11

WE HAVE NOW COME to the third extended passage dealing with the Servant of the LORD. In the first (42:1-7) the exaltation of the Servant and the success of His mission were described with no hint of discouragement or humiliation. In the second (49: 1-12) there was a brief hint of discouragement. In this third passage humiliation becomes prominent. The final passage (52:13—53:12) will describe and fully explain His humiliation and its relation to the accomplishment of His mission.

This passage reads as follows:

(4) The Lord GOD has given me the tongue of the learned, that I may know how to sustain the weary one with a word. He awakens me morning by morning; he awakens my ear to listen as those who have been taught. (5) The Lord GOD has opened my ear. I was not rebellious; I did not turn back. (6) I gave my back to the smiters, and my cheeks to those who pluck out the beard. I did not hide my face from humiliation and spitting. (7) Indeed the Lord GOD helps me; therefore I am not disgraced. Therefore I have set my face like a flint, and I know that I shall not be put to shame. (8) He who vindicates me is near. Who will contend with me? Let us stand up together. Who is my adversary? Let him come near to me. (9) Behold the Lord GOD helps me; who will condemn me? Behold they will all wear out like a garment; the moth will eat them. (10) Who among you that fears the LORD and obeys the voice of his Servant walks in darkness and has no light? Let him trust in the name of the LORD and rely on his God. (11) Behold, all you who kindle a fire, who encircle yourselves with firebrands; walk in the light of your fire and by the

**118**

brands you have kindled. This you will have from my hand; you will lie down in torment.

In this passage, as in chapter 49, the Servant Himself speaks. His soliloquy in the first person plainly continues until the end of verse 9, and seems most reasonably also to include verses 10-11.

Since the word *servant* occurs in verse 10, it is natural to think that the Servant of the LORD is the speaker. This one usage by itself might not be conclusive, since there are a few instances in the book of Isaiah where the prophet speaks of himself as God's servant; but the long series of references to the Servant in our present section and the previous appearance of the two extended passages in chapters 42 and 49 point strongly in the direction of the Servant being the speaker here. Besides, the passage hardly seems to describe Isaiah. Nowhere else in his book is there even a hint that he endured a period of suffering. Still more important, verse 11 attributes to the speaker a power far beyond anything that Isaiah would ever claim, for he says to all the faithless: "This you will have from my hand; you will lie down in torment."

It would be equally impossible for the nation of Israel to claim the power expressed in verse 11. Still greater objections to interpreting the speaker as Israel can be drawn from verses 5-6. It would not be reasonable to think of Israel as claiming to have voluntarily submitted itself to humiliation and suffering (v. 6), since it has been declared many times in our section that God caused Israel to suffer on account of its sin. Nor could we expect the prophet to attribute to Israel the words, "I was not rebellious" (v. 5), in view of the many previous statements about Israel's refusal to follow the LORD.

The passage begins with a statement, in verse 4, of the speaker's close relationship to God. Its first words parallel 49:2 in their emphasis on the ability of the Servant to speak. Christians should never cease to thank God for His priestly work in giving Himself as a sacrifice and thus making it possible that they should be saved. Yet they make a great mistake if they neglect

His prophetic work, in which He opened up the mysteries of God in the wonderful discourses included in the gospels. Here the Servant declares that God has given Him "the tongue of the learned."

The word that the King James Version rightly translates "learned"[31] is a plural noun, the form of which is clearly derived from a passive participle. It does not mean one who is learning but one who has learned or has been taught. The same word occurs at the end of the verse.

Use of the word "learned" indicates the thorough training of the Servant of the LORD. He has been trained to hear the voice of God. During His earthly life, Jesus Christ lived in a very close relationship with His Father. He said: "I do nothing of myself; but as my Father hath taught me, I speak these things" (John 8:28).

God expects Christians to learn to hear His voice, as revealed through His written Word. He has messages in the Bible for all of us. Correct understanding of His meaning requires careful study. God desires us to be able "to listen as those who have been taught."

Verses 5-6 vividly portray the humiliation of the Servant. He voluntarily submitted to suffering and death. Jesus said of His life: "No man taketh it from me, but I lay it down of myself" (John 10:18).

Verse 7 declares the Servant's determination to go through with the work assigned to Him. Jesus "stedfastly set his face to go to Jerusalem" (Luke 9:51). Though men might scorn Him, He knew that His Father would vindicate Him. This thought is developed further in verse 8. The One who will vindicate Him is near. Who then can stand against Him?

Verse 9 implies that the Servant possesses everlasting life, for He declares that His adversary will "wear out like a garment." This would be true of any mere human being. The implication is that the Servant is more than human.

These six verses have described the unique character of the Servant of the LORD and have vividly portrayed His humiliation. In the last two verses of the passage, the Servant speaks

120

directly to two groups of individuals. First He turns to those who are truly following the Lord but who, nevertheless, feel that they are walking in darkness and tend to fall into despondency. He urges such people to trust in the name of the Lord and to rely on God.

Then the Servant turns to those who are unfaithful and describes them by a unique but rather apt figure of speech. In contrast to the true followers of God, who sometimes experience difficulty in finding the light they need, He designates the faithless as "you who kindle a fire, who encircle yourselves with firebrands." Thus He points to all who trust their own wisdom instead of looking for the light that only God and His Servant can provide. Such people are ironically told that all they can do is to walk in the light of the little fires that they have kindled. Apart from what God has revealed, man can see only a a short distance in any direction. An individual with unusual mental ability may be able, through research and investigation, to peer much further into the darkness than the ordinary person. Yet even he has no basis for deciding the meaning of life or for fashioning his life in such a way that it will count for eternity.

In the final sentence the Servant of the Lord gives a more direct statement of condemnation: "This you will have from my hand; you will lie down in sorrow." To the Christian, death means only a further step in the working out of God's perfect plan. The unbeliever has no solid ground for hope beyond the grave. Death, to him, can mean nothing better than "lying down in torment."

# 8

## A Long Passage of Reassurance:
## Isaiah 51:1—52:12

THE REMAINDER of Part 2 is devoted entirely to reassurance. Even as God called Abraham and blessed him, He will continue to bless his descendants. He will cause His justice and His light to go out to all the world. He will comfort His suffering people. Just as He rescued them from Egyptian slavery and brought them safely through the Red Sea, He will free them again and destroy the oppressors. He will enable them to leave the land of Babylon and to take the vessels of the LORD back to Jerusalem. This they will do, not as fugitives, but with the full sanction of the authorities.

This summarizes the contents of this long passage. It presents no new idea but is filled with comfort and encouragement, leading up to its great climax in the actual departure from Babylonia.

This passage naturally divides into eight parts which may be grouped together as follows, noting the words with which each portion begins:

1.  a. Listen to me (51:1)
    b. Pay attention to me (51:4)
    c. Listen to me (51:7)
2.  a. Awake, awake (51:9)
    b. It it I who comforts you (51:12)
    c. Rouse yourself, rouse yourself (51:17)
    d. Awake, awake (52:1)
3.  How beautiful upon the mountains (52:7)

Verses 1-8 of chapter 51 form a poem with three stanzas. The first of these (vv. 1-3) assures those who pursue righteousness that God's promises to Abraham will not be forgotten, and declares that He will reestablish Zion as a place of joy and gladness. The second stanza (vv. 4-6) continues the universal outlook found in Isaiah 42, declaring that God will bring justice and light to all the nations, including even the distant isles, and stressing the fact that His control is universal and everlasting. The third stanza (vv. 7-8) tells those who sincerely desire to follow the Lord that they need not fear the opposition of sinful men, even though for a time these may seem to be dominant. God's people can know that in the end the wicked will be completely powerless, while His righteousness and His salvation will endure forever.

At first sight the second part of the passage appears to be another poem of three stanzas similar in structure to the first, though somewhat longer. This impression is produced by the fact that 51:9 and 52:1 begin with the words "Awake, awake," while 51:17 begins with the words "Rouse yourself, rouse yourself" (which represent a different form of the same Hebrew verb, and are translated "Awake, awake" in the King James Version). But the structure is really quite different, since verse 9 is addressed to the "arm of the Lord," while 51:17 and 52:1 are addressed to Jerusalem. This change clearly indicates that the passage begins with a prayer addressed to God and then gives the Lord's answer, thus making use of a rhetorical device found at many other points in the book of Isaiah. In Isaiah 51: 9-11 the Lord's people plead with Him to exert His power on their behalf, as He did when He delivered their ancestors from Egypt and dried up the Red Sea before them. They ask Him to allow His ransomed people to return to Zion and there to obtain everlasting gladness and joy.

Most translations render verse 11 as a prediction of the future, but in the context it seems more reasonable to consider its verbs as jussives,[32] or exhortations, translating it: "Let the redeemed of the Lord return and come with joyful shouting to

Zion; let everlasting joy be on their heads, and let them obtain gladness and joy; let sorrow and sighing flee away."

The answer to Israel's plea consists of three parts. The first is contained in verses 12-16, beginning with the words "I, even I, am he who comforts you." In verses 12-13 the LORD asks why His people should fear men, whose days are like grass, and forget the inexhaustible power of God the Creator. Verse 14 gives a specific promise: the exiles will soon be set free. They will not die in the dungeon, nor will their bread be lacking. In verses 15-16 God again calls attention to His great power over nature but declares that His power of revelation is even greater, giving His people His Word and saying to them, "You are my people."

The second part of God's answer, which begins with the words "Rouse yourself, rouse yourself," is largely devoted to describing the sufferings of Jerusalem by the figure of a mother whose sons, overwhelmed by famine and warfare, lie helpless as an antelope in a net, suffering the wrath of God. This sad description of their plight (vv. 17-20) is followed by the promise that God will take the cup of misery out of their hands and give it to their tormentors (vv. 21-23).

The third part of the answer (52:1-6) starts with words that closely parallel the beginning of the plea (51:9). There suffering Israel prayed that God's arm would put on strength. Here God assured Israel that strength is available, telling her to put it on as a garment. The parallel is even clearer in the Hebrew than in the English. Although more than twenty different Hebrew words are translated "strength" in the King James Version, the same Hebrew word[33] is used in both of these verses.

In addition to exerting His strength on Zion's behalf, God promises that she will be enabled to clothe herself in beauty and holiness. She is to be freed not only from captivity but also from uncleanness (vv. 1-2). Verse 3 gives renewed assurance that she still belongs to God. Recalling the statement in 50:1, that they were sold for their iniquities, God now declares that, just as He received no recompense when they were taken away, so also their redemption will be accomplished, not by payment of silver but through His sovereign will.

Verse 4 looks back to the Egyptian bondage and to the later Assyrian oppression which preceded the Babylonian Captivity. The Hebrew word *Ashshur* is sometimes translated "Assyria" and sometimes "the Assyrian." The name occurs more than thirty times in Isaiah 1-39, but only this once in the entire section we are now considering.

Verses 5-6 continue the note of assurance that God will free His people from their oppressors and will bring to an end the time in which His name is continually blasphemed.

The concluding portion of this long passage of reassurance is a beautiful poem reminiscent of Isaiah 40. It reads as follows:

(7) How beauitful upon the mountains are the feet of him
Who brings good news
Who publishes peace,
Who brings good news of happiness,
Who announces salvation,
Who says to Zion: Your God reigns!
(8) Listen, your watchmen lift up their voices,
Together they shout for joy;
For they shall see eye to eye when the LORD restores Zion.
(9) Break forth, shout joyfully together, you waste places of Jerusalem;
For the LORD has comforted his people,
He has redeemed Jerusalem.
(10) The LORD has bared his holy arm in the eyes of all the nations;
All the ends of the earth shall see the salvation of our God.
(11) Depart, depart, go out from there,
Touch no unclean thing.
Go out from the midst of her,
Purify yourselves, you who carry the vessels of the LORD.
(12) For you will not go out in haste
Nor will you go as fugitives,

> But the LORD will go before you
> And the God of Israel will be your rearguard.

The similarities of the first part of this poem to chapter 40 are very striking. As far as the deliverance of Israel is concerned, what was predicted there is now described as fulfilled. God announces that He has delivered His people and that they are to return safely to Jerusalem. In addition, the necessity of holiness is stressed. They must cleanse themselves from all iniquity as they leave the heartland of idolatry.

The statement in verse 11, "you who carry the vessels of the LORD," implies that the returning exiles will be able to take with them the precious articles that Nebuchadnezzar had carried away from the Jerusalem Temple. Since this could not be done if they were to escape through stealth or sudden violence, it is clearly implied that they will depart with full permission from the new authorities. God revealed in previous chapters that through His sovereign will a complete change of control would be brought about. Now that the returning exiles will be free to make the long journey homeward, partly through hostile territory and partly through long stretches of desert, God promises that He will go before them and will also protect them from attack from the rear.

The first and third lines of verse 12 begin with the preposition *ki*, which is translated into English in a variety of ways. It is frequently rendered as "for," often as "that," and sometimes as "but." There is generally some sort of causal relationship involved. The words "you will not go out . . . as fugitives" are not given as a reason to purify themselves but as an explanation of the fact that they will be able to take with them the vessels of the LORD that had been locked up in the treasure house of the Babylonian king.

Here the many promises of deliverance and return from Babylon reach their climax. This note does not occur again in our present section. A chapter division should have been placed after verse 12, instead of three verses further on.

Part 3

# The Accomplishment of the Work of the Lord's Servant

# 19

## The Servant's Atoning Work:
## Isaiah 52:13—53:12

THE REMAINDER of this section of Isaiah looks far into the future, tying together various threads that have been gradually introduced. Part 1 reached its climax in the promise that the Babylonian oppressor would be destroyed. Part 2 reached its climax in the remarkable description, given in the form of a command, of the fact that the exiles would leave Babylonia and return to Jerusalem unhindered.

In Part 1 the Servant of the LORD was introduced, and his great work of bringing light to all the world was vividly depicted. In Part 2 the individual Servant of the LORD was differentiated from the nation of Israel, and His humiliation and suffering were briefly described. Part 3 deals with the fulfillment of the promised work of the LORD's Servant, and with the results that will flow from this work.

In chapter 49 it was shown that the Servant, though from Israel, can be distinguished from the nation. He is an Israelite and represents Israel; yet He does a work for Israel as well as for the whole world.

In earlier passages the thought has been tactfully but definitely presented that Israel's suffering is the result of sin. Now the LORD tells how the sin question is to be dealt with. The extended passages about the Servant of the LORD in chapters 42 and 49 described His exaltation and the outreach of His work to the most distant nations; the passage in chapter 49 gave a hint of His humiliation and suffering, and this was clearly presented in 50:6. Now the two thoughts are to be brought together, with an explanation of the reason for His suffering and its relation to the vital problem of sin.

This first division of Part 3 is actually the climax of this entire section of Isaiah. Here we see the divine solution toward which Parts 1 and 2 have been leading. It might be called the bleeding heart of the Old Testament. No other chapter, with the possible exception of Psalm 22, gives so vivid and meaningful a presentation of the supreme factor in the entire Scripture—the promised atonement to provide salvation for all the redeemed.

It is indeed unfortunate that the chapter and verse divisions, which were put in long after Isaiah wrote, break up the thought of the passage and have thus given many readers a false impression of some of its vital factors. Many fail to realize that Isaiah 52:13-15, though far less known among Christians, is just as important a part of the passage as the material contained in chapter 53. Worse still, the mistaken verse division that combines the end of the first paragraph with the beginning of the second paragraph (along with the placing of a chapter division in the middle of this second paragraph) has caused many to gain a false impression of some of its most vital points.

Although the entire portion is a unit, it divides naturally into five parts:

1. Summary of the accomplishments of the Servant—52:13-15a (quoted on p. 131)
2. The distant outreach of the Servant's accomplishments—52:15b—53:2 (quoted on p. 133)
3. The changing perception of local observers—53:3-6 (quoted on p. 136)
4. The perfect Servant's silent submission—53:7-9 (quoted on p. 140)
5. The fulfillment of God's purpose—53:10-12 (quoted on p. 144)

It might be helpful to read these sections consecutively, with the titles in mind, before beginning the detailed discussion of each.

## 1. SUMMARY OF THE ACCOMPLISHMENTS OF THE SERVANT

(13) Behold, my servant will prosper [or, deal wisely]. He will be high and lifted up and very high. (14) Just as many were astounded at you, so marred is his appearance from that of a man, and his form from the sons of men, (15a) so he will sprinkle many nations.

The paragraph begins by saying that the Servant's work will succeed. There is no exact equivalent in English for this first verb,[33a] which contains two ideas: (1) the work will be wisely done; and (2) it will be successfully done. The same problem of translating this word occurs at many other places in the Bible (e.g., Josh 1:7; 1 Sam 18:5, 30; Jer 23:5).

The general statement of the effective accomplishment of the great work of the Servant of the LORD is followed by a description of the exaltation that would naturally result. The three verbs with almost identical meaning in the latter part of verse 13 stress the supreme nature of this exaltation and present a marked contrast to what follows.

The remainder of this paragraph shows how the work of the Servant will be done and what it will accomplish. In contrast to the Servant's exaltation, verse 14 describes His humiliation. This idea might seem very strange if it had not already been introduced in the earlier Servant passages. It will be recalled that the humiliation of the Servant was touched upon in 49:4, 7 and was extensively developed in 50:6. Here it is introduced by a comparison that is brought out much better in the Hebrew than in most translations. The verse begins with a Hebrew word that means "just as." Then the second part of verse 14 and the first part of verse 15 begin with a Hebrew particle that can express either a comparison or a result. The structure of the passage may be represented thus: "Just as————, so (similarly) ————, so (as a result)————."

Thus the statement consists of three parts. It begins with a reference to the condition of Israel in exile. Dragged away from its homeland and scattered among alien peoples, it would hardly seem any longer to be a nation. In similar circumstances many another nation has altogether lost its identity.

The verse continues by declaring that the suffering of Israel
will be paralleled by the suffering that the Servant must undergo, which will be so terrible as to make him almost seem not
to be a man. Many were horrified at the fate of Israel, so mis-
treated that it hardly seemed to be a nation; similarly many
would be appalled at the treatment of the Servant, so disfiguring
His appearance that it would hardly seem like that of a man.
This thought is brought out by the two uses of the preposition
*from*[34] (meaning "away from"), as well as by the structure of
the sentence, and by the parallel between "you"[35] in the first
clause and the reference to "his appearance" and "his form" in
the second. It is unfortunate that many translators fail to bring
out this comparison, which is so clearly indicated in the Hebrew.

The first verb in this sentence is often misunderstood. Although translated "astonished" several times in the King James
Version, this rendering is apt to give a wrong impression in today's English. The Hebrew word[35a] means that one is astounded, appalled, or horrified. It always implies something
disagreeable and is never used merely to show surprise.

Verse 15a concludes the introductory paragraph by sum-
marizing the accomplishments that will result from the Servant's humiliation. The expression "he will sprinkle many nations"[36] might not mean much to those who know nothing of
the religious observance God prescribed for the Israelites. Anyone familiar with these observances would be aware of the great
importance of ceremonial cleansing by sprinkling blood, oil, or
water. The apostle Peter showed that he understood the meaning of this verse when he wrote to the believers in many nations (1 Pet 1:1) calling them "elect . . . unto sprinkling of the
blood of Jesus Christ" (1 Pet 1:2). Thus this clause summarizes the atoning work of Christ that is so clearly presented
in Isaiah 53.

In chapters 42 and 49 it was stated that the Servant would
bring light to the nations. Attention has gradually been directed
to the fact that, important as light is, there is something else

that is far more important: deliverance from the guilt and power of sin. Such deliverance is a necessary prerequisite to bringing the promised light. By His death on the cross, Jesus suffered as a sacrifice to deliver all who would believe on Him.

The next paragraph shows that the influence of the Servant will even extend to kings of distant nations and will lead them to new and unexpected conclusions.

## 2. The Distant Outreach of the Servant's Accomplishments

(15*b-d*) Kings will shut their mouths because of him, for what had not been told them they will see, and what they had not heard they will understand. (53:1) Who would have believed what we have heard? And to whom has the arm of the LORD been revealed? (2) For he grew up before him like a tender plant and like a root out of parched ground; he had no stately form or majesty that we should look upon him, and no beauty that we should desire him.

The first clause of this paragraph shows that in the many nations to which the work of the Servant would extend, prominent leaders will have no answer to the explanation of the mystery of life that He provides. They will therefore shut their mouths on account of Him. They will see truth that is entirely new to them and completely different from anything they expected. In the remainder of the paragraph they discuss their previous incredulity.

This paragraph has been misunderstood as a result of misinterpreting the verb at the beginning of verse 14 as if it meant "astonished," and of failing to grasp the significance of the statement, "He will sprinkle many nations." As a result, the first sentence of this paragraph has been wrongly taken to mean simply that the kings were surprised. When one is surprised, however, the tendency is not to shut the mouth but to open it.

The first part of the next sentence (53:1) uses a rhetorical question to express two ideas[37]: (1) the number of those who have believed what they have heard is limited; and (2) they themselves have found it to be quite different from what they had expected. The first idea could be expressed by taking the verb as a simple perfect: "Who has believed what we have heard?" Both ideas can be expressed by translating it: "Who would have believed what we have heard?" This entirely proper way of rendering this form of the verb is required to fit the thoughts that precede and those that follow.

In the King James translation of this verse, the phrase "our report" introduces an ambiguity not found in the original, since "report" could mean either something heard or something said. The Hebrew word is the passive participle of the verb *to hear* and literally means "what we have heard." This verse is quoted twice in the New Testament (John 12:38; Rom 10:16), and in both cases a Greek word is used that is derived from the verb *to hear.* The verse is not primarily a complaint by a group of prophets lamenting that their proclamation is not being generally received, but rather an exclamation by new converts who are overwhelmed by the wonder of the salvation that has come to them.

While the primary thought here is not the fact that only a limited number will believe, that idea is definitely involved in the picture. The fact that this particular element is prominent in both New Testament quotations should not keep us from realizing that its primary meaning here is the realization that the means by which God would provide salvation is so different from what these kings of distant nations would have expected.

The verse continues with a recognition that their possession of this faith is due to the special mercy of God: "To whom has the arm of the LORD been revealed?" Thus they confess that no wisdom or goodness of their own has led them to believe the message of salvation. They believe because God, in His wonderful mercy, has revealed Himself to them.

The phrase "the arm of the LORD" has occurred several times in previous chapters to indicate God's power to save. In 51:9 the arm of the LORD was called upon to awake and help His people. In 52:10 it was declared that the LORD had made bare His holy arm in the eyes of all the nations, so that all the ends of the earth should see His salvation. This outreach of the arm of the LORD was abundantly displayed in bringing back God's people from exile (52:11-12). Here in Part 3 it is even more wonderfully active to deal with the problem of sin and to apply the results of Christ's atonement to all who will be saved.

Failure to recognize that kings, rather than prophets or actual observers, are the speakers in verse 1 has sometimes led to a complete misunderstanding of verse 2. This is particularly true of the phrases "he hath no form nor comeliness" and "no beauty that we should desire him" (KJV), which do not fit at all with the picture contained in the gospels. The character of Jesus was undoubtedly one of rare charm and attractiveness. Even the officers sent to arrest Him said, "Never man spake like this man" (John 7:46). Crowds followed Him, listening intently to His wonderful messages and wondering at the miracles He performed. It was only when it became clear that His message demanded complete and absolute allegiance that they began to fall away from Him. This verse pictures the impression the account first made on the leaders in distant nations, who expected that the answer to the problem of life might be given by a powerful Roman leader or by a great Athenian philosopher. To them, a Galilean peasant, living and dying in a little country on the very fringe of civilization, seemed like a frail plant, growing in a parched ground, altogether lacking the majesty and beauty that they would have expected to find.

In the early part of the verse, the words "before him" are important as recognizing that the Servant was always in the LORD's sight and that this seemingly frail plant derived its strength from God Himself. One who does not recognize the relation to the context might easily assume that the words "before him" are meaningless. Therefore some have suggested changing the text to read "before us"; others have gone so far as to propose breaking the word into two parts and then so altering one of them as to produce a phrase that would mean "not fair," or "not beautiful."

This paragraph has presented the reaction of leaders in distant lands. In the next, the viewpoint shifts to that of people who actually witnessed the life and death of the LORD's Servant.

135

### 3. THE CHANGING PERCEPTION OF LOCAL OBSERVERS

(3) He was despised and forsaken of men, a man of pain and acquainted with suffering; and like one from whom men hide their faces, he was despised and we did not esteem him. (4) He did indeed bear our pains and take away our diseases, yet we thought him stricken, smitten of God, and afflicted. (5) But he was wounded for our transgressions; he was bruised for our iniquities; the chastisement for our peace fell upon him, and by his scourging we are healed. (6) All of us have gone astray like sheep; each of us has turned to his own way; but the LORD has caused the iniquity of all of us to fall on him.

This paragraph begins with a closer look at the humiliation that the Servant must endure in connection with His trial and death. Those who loudly acclaimed Him shrink away; even His disciples flee in terror. He suffers the pain and misery of scourging and insult. A crown of thorns is pressed down on His head, and wicked men ridicule Him. Even Peter, who said he was ready to die for Him, denies ever having known Him. Thus verse 3 is exactly fulfilled in the suffering and death of Jesus Christ.

Verse 4 has often been misunderstood, largely because two quite specific words have been taken in a rather general sense. The Hebrew makes a sharp contrast between the first and second parts of the verse. It puts great stress on the pronoun "he" at the beginning of the first part, in contrast to a similarly emphasized "we" in the second part, thus presenting a contrast between what *he* did and what *we* thought. This contrast is further indicated by the fact that the verse begins with a Hebrew word generally translated "surely" or "truly." In the attempt to bring out the contrast more fully, this word has been rendered as "indeed" in the translation above.

The first two verbs in the verse are common Hebrew words for "carrying" or "lifting," and generally also involve the idea of removing something or taking it away. The nouns[38] used with them are literal words for physical suffering and infirmities. The King James rendering, "griefs" and "sorrows," is much too general. The clause pictures the healing ministry of

Christ. This is clearly stated in Matthew 8:16-17, where it is said that His healing works were done "that it might be fulfilled which was spoken by Esaias the prophet, saying, Himself took our infirmities, and bare our sicknesses."

In the last part of this verse, the observers confess their error. Even though they had seen His great miracles, they had completely misunderstood the situation when He was seized and killed. It grieved them that such a good man should be "stricken, smitten of God, and afflicted." This was doubtless the feeling of many who were later converted on the day of Pentecost. It was certainly true of the disciples on the road to Emmaus, as they told the Man whom they took for a stranger about their great sorrow over the death of the One whom they had seen work so many miracles and whom they had hoped would redeem Israel (Luke 24:18-21).

Jesus Himself pointed to His great miracles of healing as evidence of the truth of His claims. This is brought out clearly in John 5:36; 10:38; 14:11. Those who had seen His great miracles of healing had failed to put full confidence in His claims to be divine. Now, however, they realized that His death was not the result of divine displeasure but had an entirely different meaning, which is brought out in Isaiah 53:5.

Interpreters have sometimes read the atonement back into the first half of verse 4, translating "pains" and "diseases" in the general sense of grief, suffering, or sorrows. However, even if translated in this general way, "griefs" and "sorrows" are not a normal way of expressing the idea of sin. Many Bibles give marginal references here to Matthew 8:16-17 and 1 Peter 2:24. Actually, 1 Peter 2:24 has only one word in common with the first half of Isaiah 53:4—the word "bore." The verse gives a clear statement of the atonement of Christ and quotes from Isaiah 53:5, but it is a mistake to think of it as also quoting from verse 4.

At this point another wrong interpretation must be mentioned. It is sometimes said that the first part of Isaiah 53 describes a leper and that this is evidenced by use of the word translated "stricken."[39] It is true that this word is used in the

137

Old Testament to describe a person stricken with leprosy, but it is also employed in connection with other afflictions or injuries. Many centuries after the Old Testament was written, it came to be specialized to refer only to leprosy, but this is not true of the biblical usage. In this connection, it has been said that the reference in the previous verse to "one from whom men hide their faces" points either to the desire of a leper to hide his disfigured face or to the desire of a leper's friends not to look in his direction. While the phrase could thus describe a leper, it could equally well apply to one suffering the humiliation of being crucified. Many of Jesus' disciples fled, and even Peter denied that he knew Him. There is no reference to leprosy in this passage.

The fifth verse gives the true explanation of His suffering. The fact of the vicarious atonement is presented four times in this verse. Four times "he" and "we" are contrasted. He suffered on account of our sins. As a result of His suffering, we are healed.

The first two statements in the verse give the reason the Servant of the LORD would suffer. It was on account of our transgressions that He was wounded; it was on account of our iniquities that He was bruised.

The last two statements give the results of His suffering. The chastisement that He took upon Himself gives us peace with God and produces peace in our hearts; the scourging that He suffered makes it possible for us to be healed.

The word translated "chastisement"[40] is difficult to render in English. In the King James Version it is translated "chastening," "chastisement," or "correction" fourteen times, but is rendered as "instruction" thirty times. Once it is translated "discipline" (Job 36:10). The reader of Proverbs is told to apply his heart to instruction, to hear the instruction of his father, and not to despise the chastening of the Lord. Proverbs 4:13 says, "Take fast hold of instruction." Examination of these and other passages makes it clear that the word indicates not only something unpleasant administered by someone else, but also a discipline that one willingly takes upon himself. In our present verse it clearly indicates the great suffering that the Servant voluntarily endures in order to bring salvation to others. Jesus said: "Therefore doth my Father love me, because I lay down my life, that I might take it again. No man taketh it from me, but I lay it down of myself" (John 10:17-18).

The King James rendering, "the chastisement of our peace," literally represents the Hebrew but in present English does not quite give the thought. The Hebrew genitive does not only indicate possession but may also indicate purpose. Thus the translation "the chastisement for our peace," which brings out the thought much more clearly, is entirely proper.

The Hebrew word translated "peace"[41] means not merely cessation from warfare but actual well-being, and should be understood throughout the Bible in a much broader sense than the usual meaning of the English word *peace*.

The healing described in verse 5 is spiritual in nature. God may choose to heal us physically, but we have no right to demand that He do so. Many illnesses are caused by spiritual or mental conflicts; salvation through Christ, if properly understood and appropriated, should eliminate such conflicts and produce a mental relaxation that can relieve illnesses of this type. In any particular instance, God is able, if He chooses, to heal the body and enable the Christian to live longer than would otherwise be the case. Yet it is often His will that His people should show forth His praise by bearing patiently whatever sufferings He may choose to send them. In the present age everyone must die, but all who believe in Christ will eventually be raised from the dead, never again to suffer pain.

Verse 6 makes a very apt comparison of humanity to straying sheep. Each of us has followed his own willful desires and has strayed away from the paths that God has ordained for our good. Yet the LORD takes a particular interest in each individual, and everyone who turns to Christ can truly say that the LORD has caused his iniquity to fall on the spotless Lamb of God.

Here the portion of the chapter that uses the pronoun *we* comes to an end. The rest of the chapter is spoken from the viewpoint of the prophet looking into the future and seeing the wonderful salvation that God would provide, rather than through the mouths of those who would observe the life and death of the LORD's Servant.

### 4. THE PERFECT SERVANT'S SILENT SUBMISSION

(7) He was oppressed, and he was afflicted, yet he did not open his mouth. As a lamb being led to the slaughter, and as a sheep silent before its shearers, he did not open his mouth. (8) By oppressive judgment he was taken away. Who shall declare his generation, for he was cut off from the land of the living for the transgression of my people, to whom the stroke was due.[42] (9) His grave was assigned with wicked men, yet he was with a rich man in his death, because[43] he had done no violence and there was no deceit in his mouth.

This paragraph describes the manner of death of the LORD's Servant. Verse 7 depicts His willing submission. This verse presents a serious objection to any who would consider the Servant of the LORD as representing the entire nation of Israel. Israel was indeed oppressed and afflicted, but it could hardly be described as one who did not open its mouth but was silent before its oppressors. Israel has endured a great deal of mistreatment and suffering, but silent endurance has never been one of its characteristics.

The first words of verse 8 have been variously translated. Probably the most reasonable interpretation is to consider the words that literally read "from oppression and from judgment" as constituting a unified thought, which in English could be expressed as "an oppressive judgment." In other words, He was the victim of a judicial murder. He was not given a fair trial but was executed without any real attempt to determine what was just. This clearly fits what actually happened to Christ.

The second clause has also been variously interpreted. In the light of the remainder of the chapter, the translation contained in the King James Version seems best to fit the context, and it is certainly a possible rendering: "Who shall declare his generation?" The verb[44] is not exactly rendered by "declare"; it means rather "to muse" or "to meditate" on something. In this context, "declare" expresses the idea fairly well. It is often translated "consider," with the whole phrase rendered somewhat as follows: "Who of his generation considered that he was cut off out of the land of the living?" This rendering is quite inadmissible in view of the meaning of the verb, which occurs about twenty times in the Old Testament and is never used to mean that one interprets something as having a particular meaning.

In view of what follows it is reasonable to consider the words "Who shall declare his generation?" as a rhetorical question, meaning that since He was cut off out of the land of the living, while still a comparatively young man, the observers would expect Him to have no posterity and no continuing influence. The validity of this interpretation is illustrated by the words of the disciples on the road to Emmaus, who obviously felt that His death had ended all possibility of continuing influence or accomplishment (Luke 24:18-21).

The statement "He was cut off from the land of the living" is followed by the explanation that the cutting off was not the result of any guilt of His own; it was "for the transgression of my people." Again the thought of substitutionary atonement is clearly presented.

It should be noted that the LORD's Servant is here distinguished from "my people"—another proof that the one described is an individual, not an entire nation.

The first half of verse 9 is a remarkable prediction of an unusual circumstance that would occur in connection with the crucifixion of Christ. Here the translation in the King James Version is somewhat inaccurate. When the words are precisely translated, their relation to what occurred at the death of Christ becomes much clearer.

This is particularly true of the first clause. Here the King James Version reads, "He made his grave with the wicked." However, the verb[45] used is not ordinarily rendered as "make."

Its most common translation is "give." It is often used for appointing or assigning. As rendered in the King James Version, it sounds as if the Servant Himself made His grave. Actually the phrase is impersonal. This is a usage common in many languages but not usually expressed this way in English. Our idiom would be, "they assigned his grave" or, "his grave was assigned." The word rendered "the wicked" in the King James Version is in the plural but has no article. It is more accurate to translate it as "wicked men" and to render the whole clause "His grave was assigned with wicked men."

Since Jesus was crucified between two thieves, it would naturally be expected that He would be buried with them. The Roman custom was either to leave malefactors unburied or to disgrace them by burying a group together in an unclean place.

In the King James Version the verse continues, "And with the rich in his death." The conjunction[46] translated "and" frequently means "but" or "yet" and is often so translated in the King James Version. The idea could be expressed by "and" but is brought out more clearly when the word is translated "but." The word translated "the rich" in the King James Version is in the singular and has no article. It would be more accurately translated as "a rich man."

It was the normal expectation that the body of Jesus would be buried with the wicked men who were crucified beside Him. Yet His body, instead of being buried with them, was placed in a rich man's tomb, something that could not have occurred except as the result of an appeal by a rich man to Pontius Pilate (Matt 27:57-60). When the verse is precisely translated, it is easy to see that this prediction was exactly fulfilled in connection with the death of Christ.

Interpreters who desire to take Isaiah 53 as referring to something other than the sacrifice of Christ find a great stumbling block in the words "rich man." They say they make no sense in the context and suggest the substitution of some other word, such as *evildoers.* Yet all the manuscripts agree in the reading "a rich man." The reference in the plural to the malefactors with whom He was killed is followed by the singular of the word for "a rich man."

In the complete copy of Isaiah that was found among the Dead Sea Scrolls, the Hebrew word for "a rich man" was first written in the plural, and then the plural ending was erased. In the *Bulletin of the American Schools of Oriental Research* (February 1949), Professor Millar Burrows, of Yale University, pointed out how easily this could happen: the scribe evidently first wrote the word in the plural, under the influence of the preceding plural word for "wicked men," and then noticed that the manuscript from which it was copied had "rich man" in the singular, and therefore he erased the plural ending. Thus the Dead Sea Scrolls provide additional evidence of the accuracy of the reading "a rich man" rather than "evildoers."

This may be called an inorganic prophecy. An organic prophecy is one that predicts how God will accomplish His great purposes. An inorganic prophecy is the prediction of an incidental feature that does not seem directly to further the divine objective but merely serves as a proof that what occurs is actually the event that has been predicted. Burial in a rich man's tomb would not increase the accomplishment of the Servant in bearing the guilt of sinful humanity. It is an incidental point, mentioned seven hundred years in advance, pointing to this particular execution as the one predicted in Isaiah 53.

In the providence of God, the fact that Jesus was buried in a fine new tomb on the side of a hill was the divine means for making available convincing evidence of His resurrection. If His body had simply been cast into a felon's grave, the situation might have been quite different. The fact of the empty tomb is one of the great proofs of the resurrection.

The remainder of the verse points out how reasonable it is that One who had lived a pure life and was unjustly executed should not be buried as a criminal but should be placed in a rich man's tomb.[47] God providentially brought this about because of the Servant's spotless life and the fact that He did not at all deserve to die. The prediction of His righteousness was abundantly fulfilled in the perfect life of Jesus Christ. No other character in life, or even in fiction, has ever been completely without a flaw. No other has ever been able to ask with truth, "Which of you convinceth me of sin?" (John 8:46).

### 5. The Fulfillment of God's Purpose

(10) Yet it pleased the Lord to bruise him, putting him to grief. When he makes himself a guilt offering, he will see his seed, he will prolong his days, and the pleasure of the Lord will prosper in his hand. (11) He will see the result of the travail of his soul and will be satisfied; by the knowledge of himself will my righteous servant justify many, for he will bear their iniquities. (12) Therefore I will divide him a portion with the great, and he will divide the spoil with the strong; because he poured out himself to death, and was numbered with the transgressors, and bore the sin of many; and he will make intercession for the transgressors.

This paragraph begins with the statement that God chose that the Servant should suffer in this way. The New Testament expresses this truth by calling Him "the Lamb slain from the foundation of the world" (Rev 13:8). His death was the divine provision to atone for sin.

The second phrase in verse 10 means literally, "he made him sick."[48] It must be remembered that the Hebrew makes no distinction between a condition caused by bacteria and one produced by violence or accident. In the light of the context, the translation "putting him to grief," while rather general, is probably satisfactory.

The rest of the paragraph consists of a survey of the far-reaching results of the Servant's sacrifice. It begins with a reference to the fact that His sacrifice will be the equivalent of a guilt offering.[49] The suggestion has been made that various other sacrifices prescribed in the book of Leviticus might seem better to fit the meaning of the atonement than this particular one (called a sin offering in the KJV). The answer may well be that this offering stands here as representing the entire sacrificial system, which finds its fulfillment in the voluntary death of the Servant of the LORD.

The Hebrew particle[50] with which this part of the verse begins is usually translated "if," but need not, as the English word so often does, convey an idea of doubt. As the present context clearly teaches that the event will definitely occur, it is best to translate it as "when," as is also done in Genesis 38:9; Numbers 36:4; Judges 6:3; Psalm 78:34; Isaiah 4:4; 24:13; 28:25; and Amos 7:2.

The translation in the King James Version, "when thou shalt make his soul an offering for sin," is an equally possible translation of this phrase, as far as the Hebrew verb form is concerned, though the phrase "offering for sin" is perhaps a bit more general than the Hebrew word that the King James Version usually translates "a sin offering." Since the second-person pronoun is not used anywhere in the immediate context, there is much to be said in favor of the translation included in our text, though it is impossible to be dogmatic between the two. In either case it means that the death of the Servant represents the fulfillment of the entire sacrificial system, being the reality which it typifies in advance.

The rest of the verse describes some of the results that will follow His sacrifice of Himself. The first of these is represented by the words "he will see his seed." This statement gives a joyful answer to the rhetorical question in verse 8: "Who shall declare his generation?" The Hebrew word for "seed"[51] is often used to indicate descendants, as in the promises to Abraham. As a result of giving Himself as a guilt offering, this One who was cut off in His prime and seemed to have no prospect of leaving any permanent accomplishment will see generation after generation of those who have been brought to salvation through His sacrifice and who desire to follow Him as their Lord.

The next phrase, "he will prolong his days," shows that the Servant's activities will not end at His death. It carries a strong suggestion of physical resurrection, and this was fulfilled by Christ. The New Testament records that Jesus was raised from the dead and frequently appeared to His disciples during the next forty days. Then He ascended to heaven, where He still continues as the God-man, constantly bringing souls to salvation.

The last statement in the verse declares that by offering Himself as a guilt offering, the Servant will cause the good pleasure of the LORD to prosper. His death was not simply a way to satisfy the justice of an angry God. Though this is indeed one side of the picture, an equally important side is the fact that His death was in accordance with the plan God made far back in eternity to provide a means of salvation for sinful humanity. God the Father sent the Son to be the Saviour of the world (1 John 4:14). God so loved the world that He gave His Son to provide salvation for all who put their trust in Him. Thus the good pleasure of the LORD prospered through what the Servant did.

Verse 11 again stresses the vicarious nature of the Servant's work. It begins by referring to the suffering that He will endure on behalf of sinners, and declares that He will be fully satisfied by its results. Calvin says of this verse: "Isaiah could not have better expressed the infinite love of Christ toward us than by declaring that he takes the highest delight in our salvation, and that he rests in it as the fruit of his labors" (*Commentary on the Book of the Prophet Isaiah* [Grand Rapids: Eerdmans, 1948], 4:126).

As the verse continues, it promises that many will be justified through the knowledge of what God's righteous Servant has done, since He bore their iniquities on the cross.

In the phrase "my righteous servant," the Hebrew order is quite unusual. Literally it would read, "a righteous One, my Servant." Only One who is entirely righteous can pay the penalty for sin. None but the spotless Lamb of God can perform this great act. All others deserve death for their own sin and cannot possibly pay the penalty for anyone else.

Beginning in chapter 41, there have been many references to the LORD's Servant. After chapter 53, the word *servant* does not occur again in the singular in the book of Isaiah; instead there are a number of references to "my servants," using the plural to indicate the followers of the LORD's righteous Servant.

The phrase "will justify many" can be rendered more idiomatically in English as "will cause many to be accounted righteous." God considers all who trust in the LORD's Servant as if they had never sinned. His righteousness is imputed to us. Our iniquities are laid on Him, and it is because He bears them that we are justified.

The use of the word "many" suggests that not all of humanity will be saved, and this idea is further suggested in the statements of verse 12. As a result of the sacrifice performed by the LORD's Servant, God will "divide him a portion with the great," and He "will divide spoil with the strong." During the present age God permits Satan and his forces to control a great part of the activity of the world and to hold many of its people under their control. As a result of Christ's atonement, He will rescue many from the control of Satan and his strong and powerful forces. The three following clauses repeat the reasons the Servant can do this, and recapitulate some of the important ideas already expressed in the chapter.

Most Bible translations render the last clause of the chapter as the fourth in a parallel series. Some insert the word *yet* between the second and third so as to make two pairs of reasons. All such translations fail to indicate the fact that the fourth clause has a verb form different from the first three. The first three use the perfect tense. The fourth uses the imperfect tense, which is normally translated as a future. This difference of verb form indicates that these are not four parallel clauses. Rather, there are three clauses that belong together, followed by one of a different nature. The final clause shows the Servant's continuing activity. "He will make intercession for the transgressors." The New Testament assures us that Jesus is at the right hand of God, making intercession for us (Rom 8:34; Heb 7:25).

By His atoning death, Christ bore the guilt of all who receive Him as Saviour. Yet the impulse to sin still exerts tremendous power over believers. They should constantly seek to escape

147

its hold, but as long as they live on earth they will need divine help to grow in grace. We do not worship a dead Christ but a resurrected and living Lord. The chapter ends triumphantly, with the promise that He will constantly make intercession for the transgressors.

In concluding this discussion of Isaiah 53, attention should be called again to the fact that it is the great climactic portion of this whole section of Isaiah. It presents the solution to two great problems that were gradually brought to attention in previous chapters: (1) the problem of sin, and (2) the problem of the Servant's identity.

The first of these is the most important problem in life and was particularly important in relation to the whole question of the Exile. How can the original cause of exile be removed so that deliverance from it will be more than a mere palliation of symptoms? We have seen that the solution to this problem is summarized in the introductory paragraph to chapter 53, where it is stated that the Servant will sprinkle many nations. In this statement all the complex ceremonials of the Old Testament for cleansing from guilt and sin are gathered together in one comprehensive summary.

The general summary was followed by a description of the attitudes of distant kings and of local observers, as they came to recognize what at first seemed unbelievable, and changed from incredulity to joyful acceptance, testifying together that the Servant of the LORD had delivered them from the bonds of sin.

While sprinkling with water, blood, or oil could symbolize cleansing, an essential part of the requirement of Old Testament Law was the sacrifice of animals. At the Passover a lamb was killed with its blood placed on the door lintel of each home. There were regular morning and evening sacrifices; there were special sacrifices; there were sacrifices at recurring festivals.

Killing an animal for removal of the guilt of those who made the sacrifice was a vital part of Old Testament Law. Even a casual reading of the last four of the five books of the Law of Moses (Heb. *Torah*) gives a strong impression that sacrifice of animals to take away guilt is its most important feature. These sacrifices had no merit in themselves. They were symbols, or types, of the way God would make provision for removal of the guilt and power of sin. Forty years after these sacrifices had been fulfilled by the sufferings and death of the Messiah, they ceased to be offered. Ever since the first century of our era, large groups of pious Jews have paid great attention to fulfillment of other requirements of the biblical Law, but its most important feature—the obligation to perform the sacrifices for sin—has ceased to be observed.

The idea of vicarious sacrifice for sin is expressed four times in 53:5, and is repeated in verses 6, 8, 10, 11, and 12. There are few, if any, passages in the Bible where a single idea is repeated so many times. It is so pervasive that it cannot possibly be removed except by grossly distorting the meaning of each of these statements. All the sacrifices were fulfilled in the voluntary sacrifice of the Servant of the LORD as He gave Himself a ransom for many, so that all who put their trust in Him can find the salvation that is otherwise impossible.

The second matter that reaches a clear definition in this chapter is the identity of the Servant of the LORD. The fact that the work of the Servant of the LORD is to be performed by an individual rather than by the entire nation was suggested by the terminology of Isaiah 42 and still more strongly by that of Isaiah 49. The language of Isaiah 53 makes the individual character of the Servant absolutely clear, and this is particularly brought out in verse 8, where He is distinguished from Israel by the statement that He suffered "for the transgression of my people," thus plainly distinguishing Him from the people whose guilt He bore.

During the first ten centuries after the death of Christ, Jewish interpreters generally recognized the individual character of the Servant described in Isaiah 53. This is evident in the statements of early rabbis quoted in the Talmud or elsewhere. In the Targum (an early amplified translation into Aramaic), the passage begins with the words, "Behold my servant the Messiah" (52:13). Standard Jewish interpretation seems generally to have recognized that this chapter would be fulfilled in an individual, and the first suggestion to the contrary was probably the suggestion of the noted Jewish commentator Rashi, in the eleventh century, that the chapter describes the suffering of the entire nation.

It should be noted that the statement at the beginning of the passage, "Behold, my servant" (52:13), and the words "my righteous servant" in 53:11 tie the passage tightly together. The unity of its entire contents cannot reasonably be questioned.

# 20

## Isaiah 54

THE REMAINDER of this section of Isaiah portrays the results of the atoning work of the Servant of the LORD and adds more detail to what is summarized in 53:11, "He will see the result of the travail of his soul and will be satisfied."

Chapter 54 describes the far-reaching effects of the Servant's work in general terms. In 55:1—56:2 there is a very specific personal application to all who put their faith in the LORD's Servant. The statements in 56:3-8 show the universal outreach of the work of the Servant as God's grace is extended to people of every nation and His Temple becomes a house of prayer for all people.

The results of what the Servant did are to go on through all eternity. Much of the material in these three chapters looks forward to the very distant future. The prophet sees a beautiful vision of the glories that will come as a result of the atonement described in chapter 53. Much of its language is figurative, but its general import is usually quite clear, though some portions may not be fully understood until the time of their fulfillment.

Most of the material in these chapters describes the future blessing of all the followers of the LORD's Servant regardless of their racial or national background. In Part 3 only one small passage is devoted specifically to the nation of Israel (54:4-10). The words *Jacob, Jerusalem,* and *Zion,* so frequent in Parts 1 and 2, never occur in Part 3; and even the word *Israel* occurs only three times, in two of which it is merely part of the phrase "the Holy One of Israel" (54:5; 55:5).

Chapter 54 divides naturally into five parts, the first of which reads as follows:

> (1) Sing, O barren one, you who have borne no child; break forth into joyful shouting, and cry aloud, you who have not travailed; for the sons of the desolate one will be more numerous than the sons of the married woman, says the LORD. (2) Enlarge the place of your tent; stretch out the curtains of your dwellings; spare not, lengthen your cords, and strengthen your stakes. (3) For you will spread abroad to the right and to the left. Your descendants will possess nations, and they will people desolate cities.

These three verses are addressed to one who is described as "barren" and "desolate." She is said to have borne no child and never to have travailed. It is promised that her sons will be more numerous than "the sons of the married woman." Obviously the two individuals referred to in verse 1 are not literal women. Two suggestions have been made: (1) that the woman who has borne no children represents Israel in exile, while the married woman is Israel before the Exile; and (2) that the woman who has borne no children represents the Gentile nations, while the married woman represents Israel.

According to the first interpretation, the verse would mean that the progeny of Israel after the return from exile would be greater than the number of her children before the Exile. This interpretation mixes the figures rather badly. If Israel could be called the married woman before the Exile, the same term would certainly apply to her again when the Exile was over. The prediction that she would have more children than "the married woman" would be meaningless, since she would then be just as much a married woman as before the Exile.

An even stronger objection to this view is the fact that the woman is called "You who have borne no child." Obviously this phrase cannot be interpreted in a physical sense. No nation could be described as one who physically had borne no child, for such a nation would disappear after one generation. The reference to sons must point either to particular accomplishments or to individuals who have received great spiritual blessings. From either viewpoint, Israel would be considered as having already borne many children.

As Paul points out in Romans 9, God brought many blessings into the world through Israel. It was through Israel that the knowledge of the true God was kept alive during many centuries when the rest of the world seemed to have forgotten Him. It was through Israel that the books of the Old Testament were brought into being. It was through Israel that preparation was made for the coming of Christ into the world. From the viewpoint of having been the source from which great blessing had proceeded, Israel surely had borne many children, and had even continued to do so during the Exile, through the great revelations given through Ezekiel and Daniel.

From the other viewpoint, that of having brought into existence a spiritual progeny, Israel could also record a great accomplishment. In the centuries before the Exile there had been thousands of true believers in Israel, who had found in the sacrifices a prefiguration of the way God would provide deliverance from the guilt and power of sin. Even during the Exile there were great numbers of pious Israelites who studied the Scripture and put their faith in its promises. There was no time in Israel's history when she could properly be described as one who had borne no child. It seems quite clear, therefore, that the barren one who had borne no child is not a figure for Israel but for the Gentile nations, where darkness reigned so long.

It must be remembered that the work of the Servant is foundational to all of Part 3. This portion of Isaiah contains no specific mention of deliverance from exile but is all directly related to the work of the Servant of the LORD.

In the first long passage about the Servant of the LORD (Isa 42), His work was described as entirely related to the nations, with hardly a reference to any specific relation to Israel. In chapter 49 this emphasis was continued to a large extent, though it was specifically stated that He must also do a work for Israel (v. 6). It cannot be considered at all unlikely that the nations should be in the forefront of the discussion of the results of his work at the beginning of chapter 54.

At the beginning of chapter 41 God called all the nations before Him and declared that their idols were powerless. Here He again addresses them, promising the rich blessings that knowledge of His Servant would bring.

The prediction of the great spread of the knowledge of God among the Gentiles, so that those who were formerly barren would have even more spiritual sons than the married woman, was exactly fulfilled in the early days of the spread of Christianity. This was a development quite unexpected by the apostles when their ministry began, even though Christ had told them that they should be witnesses to Him, not only "in Jerusalem and in all Judea," but even "in Samaria and unto the uttermost part of the earth" (Acts 1:8).

Within a few decades the leaders of the Christian community, which had at first been composed entirely of Israelites, saw that a great change was occurring. The fact that the number of Gentiles who were receiving Christ was far greater than the number of Jews who recognized Him as their Messiah gave the apostle Paul much uneasiness of mind. He went so far as to say, "I could wish that myself were accursed from Christ for my brethren . . . who are Israelites" (Rom 9:3-4).

After his classic description of God's provision for justification and sanctification through Christ in Romans 1-8, Paul devoted the next three chapters to this matter. First he expressed his great concern for his own people and mentioned some of the many blessings that God had brought into the world through Israel (Rom 9:4-5). Then he declared that there is a sense in which the real Israel includes all who truly believe, rather than all who are physically descended from Abraham (vv. 6-13). His resolution of the problem was based on these three main principles:

1. God is sovereign and has a right to decide as He chooses (vv. 14-20).

2. God had predicted through the prophets that for a time Israel would be blinded and only a remnant saved (9:25-29; 10:19-21). As evidence of this, Paul quoted Deuteronomy 32:21; Isaiah 1:9; 10:22-23; 65:1-2; and Hosea 1:10; 2:23.

3. The immediate reason for so many Israelites failing to receive the Messiah is that they are trusting in their own righteousness instead of receiving in simple faith the righteousness available through Christ (Rom 9:30-33 and following).

In Romans 11 Paul declared that all this was part of God's will in order to bring salvation to the Gentiles, and he used the figure of an olive tree from which some of the branches were broken off and branches of a wild olive tree grafted in. He predicted that eventually the branches that were lopped off will be grafted back into their own olive tree, saying, "Blindness in part is happened to Israel, until the fulness of the Gentiles be come in. And so all Israel shall be saved" (Rom 11:25-26).

Though Paul did not quote Isaiah 54:1 in Romans, he had already done so in his earlier epistle to the Galatians, where he contrasted the Jerusalem that existed in his day, trying to win God's favor by obeying legalistic interpretations of the Law, with "Jerusalem which is above . . . which is the mother of us all." He pointed out that the children of the desolate, where the Word of God had previously been unknown, had become more numerous than the children of the married woman, who had sought Him by works of the Law instead of by faith (Gal 4:25-27).

Thus we can see that Isaiah 54:1-3 is a prediction of the outreach of the atoning work described in Isaiah 53 to those who had previously been in darkness.

Verses 2 and 3 describe the extension of the work of the LORD's Servant as the message is carried to distant areas of the world. Verse 2 is the great text on which William Carey preached when he urged that a mission be formed to take the Gospel to India. Carey was not taking a few Bible words out

155

of their context in order to fit his ideas; he was interpreting the verse exactly in agreement with the thought of the passage as a whole, with its wonderful promise of worldwide extension of the knowledge of what the LORD's Servant would do at Calvary.

In verse 3 the promise is given that the message will be carried in all directions. As a result, the descendants of the one who was formerly barren but who has now received salvation will possess nations and people cities that were formerly desolate, as far as any knowledge of the true God was concerned.

After verse 3 the speaker ceases to direct his attention specifically to the one who had borne no child and instead addresses the married woman:

> (4) Do not fear, for you will not be put to shame. Do not feel humiliated, for you will not be disgraced. You will forget the shame of your youth and will no longer remember the reproach of your widowhood, (5) for your Maker is your husband; the LORD of Hosts is his name; and your Redeemer is the Holy One of Israel. He will be called the God of the whole earth. (6) For the LORD has called you, like a wife forsaken and grieved in spirit, even like a wife of one's youth when she is rejected, says your God. (7) For a brief moment I forsook you, but with great compassion I will gather you. (8) In an outburst of anger I hid my face from you for a moment; but with everlasting loving-kindness I will have compassion on you, says the LORD your Redeemer. (9) This is like the waters of Noah to me, when I swore that the waters of Noah should not flood the earth again; so I have sworn that I will not be angry with you nor rebuke you. (10) For the mountains may depart and the hills be removed, but my lovingkindness will not be removed from you, and my covenant of peace will not be taken away, says the LORD who has compassion on you.

The difference between this passage and the preceding one is very great. Its first two verses show clearly that a different person is being addressed. She is called a "wife of one's youth" (v. 6) who has suffered "the reproach of widowhood" (v. 4) and has been rejected for a time but is now to be restored. The period of God's anger is spoken of as "a brief moment" (vv. 7-8), and she is assured that the LORD is her Husband (v. 5), who will show her everlasting kindness (v. 8). These verses clearly refer to Israel as a nation, rejected for a time because of her sin, but ultimately to be restored.

The great promise of God's continuing love (vv. 9-10) can be appropriated by all who are saved through the work of the Servant, though it applies in a special sense to the descendants of Israel.

The next two verses use an entirely different figure of speech.

> (11) O afflicted one, storm-tossed, and not comforted, see, I am setting your stones in antimony, and I will lay your foundations in sapphires. (12) I will make your pinnacles of rubies, your gates of crystal, and your entire wall of precious stones.

Here the future glory of God's people is pictured under the figure of a great building of marvelous beauty formed largely of precious stones. The passage does not clearly indicate what the building represents, but the context strongly suggests that it is a figurative picture of all the followers of the Servant of the LORD joined together in one body, as described in Ephesians 2:11-22, forming a great edifice, of which Christ is the chief cornerstone (Eph 2:20-22).

In the next part the division between verses 13-14 has been badly placed. The first clause of verse 14 goes with verse 13, but the rest of verse 14 belongs with the succeeding verses.

> (13) All your sons will be taught by the LORD, and the well-being of your sons will be great. (14a) In righteousness you will be established.

This is a marvelous picture of God's promise for the spiritual well-being of the followers of the LORD's Servant. Its complete fulfillment looks far beyond the present time, but it has been partly fulfilled during the centuries since Isaiah wrote. God has given His entire revelation in the sixty-six books of the Bible, which are His instruments for teaching His people. Righteousness, based on the Bible, is the only secure foundation for any nation. A nation that bases its life on the Bible can look forward to prosperity and will be established in righteousness. This has been fulfilled many times in the history of God's people.

The remainder of chapter 54 reads as follows:

> (14b-c) You will be far from oppression, for you will not fear, and from terror, for it will not come near you. (15) On occasions when someone continually stirs up strife, it will not be from me; the one who strives with you will fail because of you. (16) Behold, I am the one who created the smith that blows the fire of coals and brings out a weapon for its purpose, and I have created the destroyer to lay waste. (17) No weapon that is formed against you will prosper; and you will condemn every tongue that rises against you in judgment. This is the heritage of the servants of the LORD, and their righteousness is from me, says the LORD.

This portion of the chapter looks at the miseries of God's people and declares that they need not fear. Troubles will come, but God will not Himself cause them. The prophet's vision looks into situations far beyond his time, and it is difficult to pinpoint precisely the time of fulfillment. In principle, the passage has found expression in the lives of all who recognize the suffering Servant as their Saviour and also, to a very definite extent, in the experience of the descendants of the people of Israel.

In verse 15, our translation, "continually stirs up strife," differs from that found in most Bibles but is equally possible from the Hebrew[52] and fits the context somewhat better.

The promise that terror "will not come near" has never yet been fully realized. Almost every group of God's people has had to go through periods of oppression and fear. This passage promises that such oppression will not go on indefinitely. Sometimes it is produced by Satan; in many cases it results from sin. Yet God uses it for His own purposes in developing His people, and He promises that eventually He will bring it to a complete end. Although verse 15 recognizes that there will be times when God's people will undergo prolonged opposition, it declares that their assailants will eventually fall and that God's purposes will triumph in and through His people.

In verse 16 God states that no one can build instruments of destruction without His permission and that He will use even the forces of evil as instruments to accomplish His purposes. This verse summarizes the teaching about God's relation to the Assyrians that is presented in Isaiah 10:5-15.

The first part of verse 17 promises that every weapon formed against God's people will eventually fail and that everyone who attacks them will eventually be overthrown.

The fact that two separate sentences are included in this one verse can easily give the false impression that the last half of the verse merely summarizes the first half. Actually, the final sentence summarizes the entire chapter, saying that this is the heritage of the servants of the LORD and belongs to them because of what the LORD's Servant accomplished, as described in Isaiah 53. As a result of what the Servant has done, His followers, here called "the servants of the LORD," will receive a marvelous heritage, including the general blessings described in this chapter and the individual blessings described in the next two chapters.

The King James translation of the final words of this verse, "their righteousness is of me,"[53] can easily give a false impression. The Hebrew uses a very emphatic preposition which combines the two words *from* and *with,* thus clearly pointing to God as the source and origin of the righteousness mentioned. In view of the full statement in chapter 53 of the foundation on which all true righteousness must be based, we can reasonably consider these words a clear statement of the fact that justification of God's people must originate with Him and is not produced by any accomplishment of man. God imputes His righteousness to those who are saved through Christ. Thus the chapter ends with a positive declaration that justification is only by faith.

At this point the Revised Standard Version says "vindication" instead of "righteousness."[54] This reading may be proper in certain contexts but is quite out of place here. The word very definitely means "righteousness," as is clear in dozens of occurrences. There are places where it indicates the fact that one's righteousness has been established or that attacks upon it have been proven to be false. It is only in such contexts that it can properly be rendered as "vindication."

# 21

## The Gracious Invitation: Isaiah 55:1—56:2

AFTER THE GENERAL STATEMENT in chapter 54 of the out-reach of the results of the sacrifice performed by the LORD's Servant, the first part of chapter 55 deals specifically with these results as they relate to individuals. The language of this chapter is as wide as all humanity. To be eligible for the indescribable blessings provided through the Servant's work it is only necessary that one recognize his need.

The chapter divides naturally into groups of two verses each, except that the first part of verse 3 goes with what precedes, while its latter half clearly belongs with what follows.

> (1) Ho, every one who thirsts, come to the waters; and all who have no money, come, buy and eat. Come, buy wine and milk without money and without price. (2) Why do you spend money for that which is not bread, and your labor for that which does not satisfy? Listen carefully to me; eat what is good and delight yourselves in fatness. (3) Incline your ear and come to me. Listen, that your soul may live.

This is one of the greatest Gospel calls to be found anywhere in the Scripture. The note of universality is struck right in the first line. It is addressed to all who thirst. It declares that God's inexhaustible blessings are available to everyone who will receive them.

Verse 1 stresses the fact that the wonderful gift is offered freely. Yet these verses must be understood in relation to Isaiah 53. Although the human recipient pays nothing for what is offered, it cost the divine Giver a tremendous amount. In order to provide this free salvation it was necessary that He pay an infinite price—the death of His one, unique Son.

Ponce de Leon spent the last part of his life searching through the wilds of Florida, hoping vainly to find the fountain of youth. His tremendous longing was never satisfied. These verses offer something far better than the fountain of youth. The soul of anyone who responds to this gracious invitation can "delight [itself] in fatness."

The terminology of these verses is somewhat figurative and quite general in character. The word "thirst" does not refer simply to need of physical water. Even those with a great abundance of this world's goods may have a tremendous thirst. Verse 2 points out the folly of the people of the world as they struggle to obtain things that can never satisfy.

The invitation looks forward to Jesus' words to the woman of Samaria: "Whosoever drinketh of this water shall thirst again: but whosoever drinketh of the water that I shall give him shall never thirst; but the water that I shall give him shall be in him a well of water springing up into everlasting life" (John 4:13-14).

The word *come* occurs three times in verse 1 and once in verse 3. God provides salvation freely for everyone who thirsts, but He calls upon sinners to come. In verses 2 and 3 He urges them to listen. Man is not a mere automaton. Life is real. Decisions are real. Man has to make choices and is responsible for the choices he makes. God has made man a rational and moral creature, and expects him to use his mind and govern his will.

This passage gives full warrant for pleading with sinners to receive the salvation that Christ procured through His sacrifice at Calvary. The urgency of the invitation can be compared to our Lord's parable in which He described a householder as ordering his servants to go "out into the highways and hedges, and compel them to come in" (Luke 14:23).

The call to listen carefully is very important. God has given His people the duty, not simply of proclaiming the message of salvation, but of pressing it upon sinners and urging them to listen carefully in order to understand the unbelievable riches of His marvelous offer.

The next passage begins in the middle of verse 3:

> (3c) And I will make an everlasting covenant with you, even the sure mercies of David. (4) Behold, I have given him as a witness to the peoples, a leader and commander to the peoples. (5) See, you will call a nation you do not know, and nations that have not known you will run to you because of the LORD your God, even the Holy One of Israel, for he has glorified you.

The invitation is followed by assurance that the blessings promised are not temporary but permanent. This was already suggested in the statement, "that your soul may live." Here the Lord promises that He will make an everlasting covenant with all who answer His gracious invitation. In the physical matters of life one may feel completely satisfied for a time, but a few hours later he will hunger and thirst again. Psychological stresses and strains often produce a feeling of dissatisfaction or uncertainty; but the one who has received the gift promised in this chapter has a right to say, "God has established an everlasting covenant with me. No matter how I may feel, I can know that He has given me the wine and milk I need. I should turn away from the merely temporary things of this world and let my soul delight itself in fatness."

The promised covenant is described as "the sure mercies of David." There are three problems involved in the translation of this phrase. The first relates to the word rendered "sure" in the King James Version and "faithful" in the *New American Standard Bible*. This Hebrew word[55] literally means "made firm." It is related to the word *amen,* with which prayers are concluded.

The second problem concerns the word that is translated "mercies" hundreds of times in the King James Version.[56] Most modern translations tend to render it "loving-kindnesses" or "steadfast love." It goes far beyond our modern word *mercy,* but the element of forgiveness and compassion is involved in it, as well as the element of continuing benevolence. We have ordinarily translated it "loving-kindness," but in this context, "mercy" seems especially appropriate.

The third problem is the relation of the phrase to what precedes. The King James Version inserts the word "even" in italics to show that the phrase is in apposition with what precedes. Some modern translations insert the words "according to," thus reducing the relation to David to a mere analogy. If it were not for the next verse, this would seem to be a reasonable interpretation, since God's mercy to David is an excellent example of the mercy He extends to all who put their trust in the merits of His Son.

The sure mercies given to David were visible at point after point in his life. He was not a man who had any righteousness of his own for which he could claim God's favor. He forgot God and fell into grievous sin, but he always came back, confessing his sin and seeking God's mercy. David is an outstanding example of the fact that salvation is by faith, apart from any works of the Law. He could well have said, "Nothing in my hand I bring, simply to Thy cross I cling." David wrote Psalm 51, expressing the anguish of the one who has sinned against God and knows that he deserves eternal punishment for his sin. Yet God gave David the great joy that belongs to those who have repented of their sin and received God's unstinting mercy with a full heart. The relation of God to those who receive the Gospel invitation of verses 1-3 is similar to His mercies to David, but this is not the primary thought of the verse. The phrase "the sure mercies of David" is in apposition with the words "an everlasting covenant."

Proof that this is what the phrase means here is provided by the next verse, which otherwise would seem to represent a complete change of thought. David is not merely a prototype of the life of the one who recognizes that all that he has been struggling for is that which is not bread and which does not satisfy. He is actually an instrument in establishing God's marvelous covenant. It is the faithful promises to David that are here in view. David was a great witness to God's mercy and was also a leader and commander of God's people. **David's** greater Son is the great Witness and the great Leader and **Commander** of all who are redeemed through the work of the LORD's Servant described in Isaiah 53.

David was a leader and commander of many peoples. He extended Israelite control over a far larger area than at any other time in its history. David's greater Son is to be a Leader and Commander of the peoples of the entire world. In modern English, the word "peoples" is not often used. The Hebrew form used here[57] is plural to indicate that many nations are involved.

Verse 5 shows that the outreach of the work of the Servant will not only involve an extension of sway over many peoples, but will involve a willing seeking on the part of many to receive the blessings of the sure mercies of David. Nations that have never heard of Israel will come. The passage is reminiscent of Isaiah 2:3, with its promise that many peoples will come to Zion to hear the word of the LORD.

> (6) Seek the LORD while he may be found; call upon him while he is near. (7) Let the wicked man forsake his way and the unrighteous man his thoughts; and let him return to the LORD, and he will have compassion on him; and to our God, for he will abundantly pardon.

These two verses continue the glorious offer of free salvation stressed in verses 1-2 but introduce three ideas not previously mentioned. The first is found twice in verse 6, with its call to seek the LORD "while he may be found." Here there is a definite implication that God will not always be available, and also a reminder of the fact that this offer was not extended to the nations of the world before the great work of the Servant was actually performed. When Paul addressed the Athenians he said: "The times of this ignorance God winked at; but now commandeth all men every where to repent" (Acts 17:30).

Only rarely before the coming of Christ were members of other nations invited to believe in the true God. After Jesus was raised from the dead He explicitly commanded that the message be carried to all the nations of the world. Now is the day of salvation. These verses imply that a time will come when it will no longer be available. For some the return of Christ will mean the beginning of a new and joyous existence. For others it will mean the end of all opportunity to accept God's gracious invitation.

The second note mentioned here that was not contained in verses 1-2 is the requirement that the wicked man forsake his way and the unrighteous man his thoughts. The order of these two passages is important. Man is not first told that if he will forsake his way and leave his thoughts God will have mercy on him. In verses 1-2 he is told that he may drink the water of life freely, in view of what Christ has done. In verses 6-7 it is made clear that the one who accepts this gracious invitation will be expected to leave his ungodly thoughts and change his ways. No man can do this in his own strength. The power promised in verses 1-2 is necessary first.

The third note in these verses that was not contained in verses 1-2 is the specific emphasis on pardon of past sins. Some come to Christ because of a great feeling of guilt and need of pardon; others are won through the gracious invitation and then come to realize their guilt and seek the pardon that God so freely offers through what the Servant accomplished at Calvary.

> (8) For my thoughts are not your thoughts, neither are your ways my ways, says the LORD. (9) For as the heavens are higher than the earth, so are my ways higher than your ways and my thoughts than your thoughts.

These verses are not a statement of the Barthian view that God is "so altogether other" that no one can really know Him. For proper understanding, they must be considered in relation to verse 7. God promises abundantly to pardon men who have turned their back on their Creator and cast aside His righteous Law. This is something that no mere human being could do. These verses show the contrast between God's loving character and the attitude of human beings who have not been changed by the regenerating power of Christ.

(10) For as the rain and the snow come down from heaven, and do not return there without watering the earth and making it bring forth and bud, and giving seed to the sower and bread to the eater, (11) so shall my word be that goes forth from my mouth; it will not return to me empty, but it will accomplish what I desire, and will succeed in the thing for which I sent it.

All of God's actions are purposeful. The creation and development of the universe are not an accident. God has a marvelous and perfect plan, and His desires will certainly be accomplished.

In addition to this great general truth, these verses show the special importance of the word that goes forth from God's mouth—which finds its greatest expression in the sixty-six books of the Old and New Testaments. The Bible has had an influence in human life far beyond that of any other book. Many have come to the truth simply by reading it, without hearing it explained by another human being. It is not only a presentation of truth; it is a presentation with power and effectiveness, constantly used by God to accomplish His purposes.

(12) For you will go out with joy, and be led forth with peace. The mountains and the hills will break forth into singing before you, and all the trees of the field will clap their hands. (13) Instead of the thorn the cypress will come up, and instead of the brier the myrtle will come up, and it will be to the LORD for a memorial, for an everlasting sign that will not be cut off.

These two verses present the great climax of God's work. It will result in joy and peace. All the universe will sing together with happiness over the results of what Christ did on the cross. All the evil that sin has brought will be removed. The thorns and briers that were introduced when men fell will be replaced by plants that are strong and beautiful.

Verse 13 beautifully illustrates the changes that should occur in the lives of all who come to know Christ. In their character the thorn bush should be replaced by the cypress and the brier

167

by the myrtle tree. The everlasting life that they receive through what Christ did on the cross is an everlasting sign that will not be cut off.

Yet this figurative interpretation could hardly exhaust the meaning of the verse. In connection with statements elsewhere in Isaiah and in other parts of the Bible it clearly states that God will remove the curse that was laid upon the world when Adam sinned, and will bring it back to its Edenic condition.

Since chapter 55 comes to a great climax in its last two verses it might seem reasonable to leave 56:1-2 for consideration with the verses that follow them in chapter 56. Yet, as does so much of chapter 55, 56:1 uses the second person, being addressed to those whom the LORD calls. These two verses have far more in common with chapter 55 than with the remaining verses in chapter 56. We shall therefore consider 55:1—56:2 as a unit.

> (1) Thus says the LORD, Preserve justice and do righteousness, for my salvation is about to come and my righteousness to be revealed. (2) Blessed is the man who does this, and the son of man who takes hold of it; who keeps from profaning the Sabbath, and keeps his hand from doing any evil.

While it may seem like an anticlimax for these practical statements to follow the great climax in verses 12-13, their presence here is a reminder that the believer who has been freed from the guilt of sin must still seek God's help to overcome its power. Sanctification is sometimes a rather slow process. It is vital that every believer endeavor always to keep his eyes on the LORD and to follow His righteous commands.

# 22

## The Universal Outreach: Isaiah 56:3-8

THESE SIX VERSES form a fitting conclusion to the section of
Isaiah that we have been studying.

> (3) Let not the foreigner who has joined himself to the LORD
> say, The LORD will surely separate me from his people. Let
> not the eunuch say, Behold, I am a dry tree. (4) For thus
> says the LORD, To the eunuchs who keep my sabbaths, and
> choose the things that please me and take hold of my covenant,
> (5) to them I will give in my house and within my walls a
> place and a name better than that of sons and daughters. I
> will give them an everlasting name that will not be cut off.
> (6) Also the foreigners who join themselves to the LORD, to
> serve Him and to love the name of the LORD, to be His serv-
> ants, everyone that keeps the sabbath from polluting it and
> takes hold of my covenant, (7) I will bring these to my holy
> mountain and make them joyful in my house of prayer. Their
> burnt offerings and their sacrifices will be acceptable on my
> altar, for my house shall be called a house of prayer for all
> peoples. (8) The Lord GOD, who gathers the dispersed of
> Israel, proclaims, I will gather to him still others, along with
> those already gathered.

In order to keep alive the knowledge of the true God and to
prepare the way for the coming of His Son, it was necessary for
a time that God keep Israel strictly separate, while leaving
most of the other peoples of the world outside. Now that the
great atonement has been performed, as described in Isaiah 53,
such barriers can be dropped. In accordance with Paul's analogy in Romans 11, the wild olive branches are grafted into the
olive tree of God's true people. The stranger, with no back-

ground or ancestry among those who knew the LORD, is not to be left out. Every eunuch was forbidden to enter the congregation of Israel (Deut 23:1), and neither a bastard nor the son of a bastard could do so until the tenth generation (Deut 23:2). Now eunuchs who take hold of God's covenant are told that they will be given a name even better than that of sons and daughters. In view of what Christ has done, all who love the name of the LORD will be accepted. God will bring them to His holy mountain, and His house will be called a house of prayer for all peoples.

The last three verses of chapter 56 are completely unrelated to its earlier portion. A new section of Isaiah's book begins at 56:9. The following chapters have little in common with the section that we have been studying but have a greater affinity to earlier parts of the book. Toward the end of the final section a closer relation to the section that we have been studying begins to appear, with a definite relation to the material we have just been discussing. There are eight references to the servants of the LORD in chapters 65-66, all of which point back to Part 3 of the section to which the present writing is devoted.

Thus we have sketched the development of thought in this great section of Isaiah that runs from Isaiah 40 to 56:8. Truly it can be called the "Gospel of Isaiah."

These chapters have illustrated the way God reveals His truth, gradually leading His people to an understanding of its deeper meanings. Starting with a summary of the great promise of redemption, the prophet soon turned his attention to the problems immediately confronting the Israelites, and gradually led them to realize that all their difficulties are related to the central problem of sin. Though deliverance from the misery of exile was wonderfully promised, glimpses were given from time to time of eventual glories that would come to God's people. The Servant of the LORD was introduced briefly. Then the great outreach of His work was sketched. Gradually it was shown that He must be an individual who is of Israel and who can represent Israel in carrying out its responsibility, but who is able to accomplish what only God Himself can do. In Part 3 the consummation of His task was portrayed, as He would make atonement for sin and begin His great work of intercession. The picture of divine redemption ended with the glorious Gospel call of chapter 55 and the assurance in chapter 56 that God's Kingdom is open to all people, regardless of physical ancestry or racial background.

# Appendix

## NOTE 1: TRANSLATION

IN THIS VOLUME all quotations from any part of the Bible except Isaiah 41:1—56:8 are taken from the King James Version. All quotations from this section represent the author's translation from the Hebrew, unless otherwise identified.

Since the emphasis of the book is primarily on interrelation of passages and ideas rather than on minutiae, most of the ideas expressed can be understood in connection with almost any translation of this part of Isaiah. Wherever any important thought rests on a particular interpretation of a Hebrew word or phrase, that fact is stated either in the text or in an Appendix note.

It was necessary for the author to make his own translation of the passages that are particularly discussed in this book for two reasons.

1. Although most of the King James Version is a very accurate translation and some parts of it are more accurate than many of the recent translations, yet it uses numerous forms and expressions that are not in common use today. In some instances, the meaning of an English word has so changed in 300 years that it now gives an impression quite different from what the King James Version translators intended. As a result, the average person will often get a better understanding of the meaning of the Bible by using one of the newer translations.

2. The translators of a number of excellent recent versions of the Old Testament, though good scholars, were not particularly aware of the principles of interrelationship and in-

terpretation that are brought out in this book. There are many points where either of two renderings would be equally accurate as far as an individual sentence is concerned. In such cases they sometimes use a rendering that does not clearly bring out the thought of the verse in relation to its context. Though some of these versions are doubtless superior, from a literary viewpoint, to the author's translation, he believes that in this section his own renderings give a more accurate presentation of the meaning of the verses in relation to their context.

A person who knows only one language is not likely to be aware of the complexity of problems involved in translation. Some of these, which relate to the meaning of verb forms and constructions, are briefly discussed in Appendix Note 2. Something should be said here about problems relating to the translation of individual words.

It is rare in any language for a word to represent a point; usually a word represents an area of meaning. In various languages these areas of meaning differ from each other, and even within one language they change over a period of time. Thus in the English of 300 years ago the word *meat* meant any kind of food. The statement in Ezekiel 47:12 that the fruit of the tree was for meat may impress a modern reader as ludicrous, since we now restrict the use of the word *meat* to what at that time would have been called "flesh." There are many places in the Bible where the word *meat,* as used by the King James Version, is entirely accurate. There are other cases where it is quite inaccurate, as far as modern English is concerned. Since the area covered by words differs from language to language, the area of meaning of an English word will often overlap but not exactly coincide with the area of meaning of a Hebrew word. As a result there will be certain contexts in which one translation would be correct but other contexts in which it would be incorrect; conversely, the English word may include ideas that are not in the Hebrew word.

A century ago it was common among students of language

to think that the meaning of a word could be proved by finding the meaning of a similar word in a related language. Commentaries often based arguments about the meaning of Hebrew words on similar words in Arabic. This method has now been almost entirely abandoned by competent linguists, as it is recognized that while such similarities may suggest possibilities of interpretation, only usage can prove a meaning.

Words often develop in very different ways in related languages. For instance, the English word *knight* and the German word *knecht* have the same origin but have developed very differently. In German, *knecht* means a servant; in English, *knight* indicates a man of rather high standing.

If a word occurs a number of times in the Old Testament it is usually easy to determine its meaning from the context. If it occurs only once or twice it is more difficult, since practically all the ancient Hebrew that has been preserved is in the Old Testament. In such cases the meaning of a similar word in a cognate language may suggest possibilities but cannot prove them. Help is also gained by comparing related words in Hebrew and by examining the way the word has been rendered in ancient versions (see Note 3).

### Note 2: Peculiarities of the Hebrew Language

Since it is necessary, in studying the book of Isaiah, to refer to particular features of the Hebrew language, an explanation of some of these features will be given at this point.

The Hebrew verb system does not possess the great precision and flexibility of the Greek verb system, or even as much as is available in the English language. Aside from the imperative, infinitives, and participles, Hebrew has only two tenses. The perfect tense represents an action as completed, while the imperfect tense presents an action as it occurs. Either of these tenses may be used to express situations in past, present, or future, though in the majority of cases the perfect can safely be translated as past and the imperfect as future. Many future events predicted in the prophetic books are considered as so definite that they are represented as already accomplished and therefore use the perfect tense, which is then called "the prophetic perfect." In the Old Testament, a perfect or imperfect verb is often introduced by a conjunction, called *"waw* consecutive," that has the effect of changing the usage of imperfect into perfect and vice versa.

It is often difficult to be certain how to express a particular Hebrew verb in English, as far as tense is concerned; but when one or more Hebrew verbs using a certain tense are followed by one that uses the other tense, as at the end of the last verse of Isaiah 53, one must consider that there is a definite reason for the change.

A peculiarity of Semitic languages such as Hebrew is that a verb may appear in various "stems." Hebrew has seven fairly common stems. The significance of each stem may vary with different words. In general it may be said that the *qal* stem represents the simple idea of a verb, although there are instances where this idea is carried by the *niphal* rather than the *qal*. Otherwise the *niphal* may represent a reflexive idea or may take the place of a passive for the *qal*.

The *hiphil* stem usually expresses the idea of leading someone to perform an act or causing it to be performed.

The *piel* is generally called an intensive but frequently expresses a causative idea. Thus the *qal* of *lāmadh* means "learn"; in the *piel* it means "teach," or "cause to learn."

The *pual* and *hophal* are the passives of the *piel* and the *hiphil*.

The other rather common stem is called the *hithpael*.

The *qal* has both an active and a passive participle. Other participles are active or passive depending on the nature of the stem with which they are connected.

Early Hebrew does not have a word corresponding to the English verb "to be." Instead it simply places two nouns or a noun and an adjective next to each other, and some form of the copula is understood. Thus wherever a translation of Isaiah includes a form of the verb "to be," it could have been translated "is," "was," or "will be," depending on the context.

## Note 3: Ancient Versions

In interpreting any part of the Bible, it is useful to consult early translations (generally called "versions"). The earliest of these is the Septuagint (often represented by *LXX*), a translation into Greek in the second century before Christ. Another very important version is the Vulgate, translated from Hebrew into Latin by Jerome about A.D. 400.

Another ancient version of value is the so-called Targums. These are translations into the Aramaic language, made by Jews in the early centuries of the Christian era. It is probable that they were preserved orally for a long time before being written down, and that they originated from oral translations given in the synagogue after the Hebrew was read, as most of the Jews then spoke Aramaic rather than Hebrew. Since the desire was not simply to translate but also to interpret, the Targums are generally not an exact translation. Yet they give valuable help, particularly in connection with the use of rare words. They are of special interest for understanding early Jewish exegesis. Thus the Targum of Isaiah 52:13 begins with a reference to "my servant the Messiah."

Other translations were made by Christians into Syriac, a dialect of Aramaic. There are fragments of two manuscripts representing a very early translation into Syriac, but most of the Syriac manuscripts contain the so-called Peshitto, which most scholars now consider as having been made at about A.D. 400.

## Note 4: The Unity of Isaiah

In recent years it has been widely taught that this portion of Isaiah was not written by Isaiah but by an unknown prophet who lived shortly before the end of the Exile. This claim rests on three types of argument: historical, literary, and theological. The historical argument is based on the fact that the section assumes exile as already present; Jerusalem as already destroyed; the Babylonians, rather than the Assyrians, as the oppressing nation; and it even refers to Cyrus by name. As pointed out on pages 18 to 22, the general facts of exile were amply familiar to Isaiah's followers, since the Northern Kingdom had already gone into exile. Just before the beginning of this section of his book, Isaiah had explicitly predicted that Judah would be captured by the Babylonians rather than by the Assyrians (Isa 39: 5-7). Use of the name *Cyrus* requires belief in a supernatural God who could reveal a fact long before it occurred. Anyone who believes in such a God should have no difficulty in believing that He could reveal these facts to Isaiah, or that He could lead Isaiah to write in such a way that he would not only bring comfort to his godly followers but precisely meet the need of those Israelites who would live as exiles in Babylonia a century later.

This historical argument is the basic one. Once it is solved, it is easy to see that the difference in subject matter is sufficient to account for differences of literary style or theological emphasis. Anyway, these differences are far less than the very marked similarities in these regards between this and other sections of Isaiah. One critic has gone so far as to say that "the second Isaiah" seems almost to be Isaiah returned from the dead! To the believer in an inerrant Bible, the fact that the New Testament quotes this section as well as the earlier part of the book as being the words of Isaiah would seem to settle the matter (cf. Rom 10:16, 21; 9:27, 29).

## NOTE 5: THE INEFFABLE NAME OF GOD

Wherever the word *Lord* is written in capital and small capital letters it represents the ineffable name of God. This name is written with the consonants YHWH, but its exact pronunciation is unknown, since the Jews stopped pronouncing it before the time of Christ (though it formed the first part of such proper names as *Jehoiakim* and *Jehoshaphat* and the last part of such names as *Hezekiah* and *Adonijah*). Long before the time of Christ the custom developed of reading the common word *Lord* wherever this name appeared. When the vowel marks were inserted in manuscripts, probably about the tenth century after Christ, the original consonants were copied, but the vowels of the ordinary word *Lord* were inserted, and that word was read instead of the consonants that were actually written. The ordinary Hebrew word for *lord* is used for God a few times in the Old Testament, but it is used far more frequently for human beings in positions of authority. The King James Version indicated this distinction by writing the word in capital and small capital letters when it represents the divine name, and that distinction has been preserved in this book.

# Notes to Particular Points

1. Hebrew ṣūlā
2. Hebrew mᵉṣūlā
3. The form is *piel*. The *niphal* of *nāḥam* means "to be comforted." The *piel* means "give comfort," or "cause one to be comforted."
4. The Hebrew word *kephel* is derived from a root *kāphal*, meaning "to fold over," as of a curtain so folded over that each part is equal to the other. The rather common idea of "twice as much" is generally expressed in Hebrew by *mishneh* or *shᵉnayim*.
5. "Proclaim," Hebrew *qārā*
6. In Isaiah 40:10 the Hebrew word *pᵉʿullā* is derived from the common verb "to do" and is properly translated "work," as in the King James Version. Only once is it used for "wages," and there it denotes the result of work. Usually it is a mistake to translate it as "recompense" or "reward."
7. The Hebrew *ʾiyyīm*, which occurs frequently in this section of Isaiah, has no exact equivalent in English. As used in the Old Testament it refers to the distant regions bordering the Mediterranean Sea, so either "isles" or "coastlands" is only a rough translation.
8. Many recent translations insert the preposition *from* before "the foundations." Two grounds are presented for this, as follows:
   1. It is said that the parallel with the previous clause requires it. Yet synonymous parallelism, though common in Hebrew poetry, is by no means universal. The second of two parallel lines often adds to the thought of the first. Thus verse 24 begins with three parallel clauses, the first two of which are synonymous, but the third takes a step further in the thought. It continues with two parallel lines, the second of which carries the thought very definitely beyond the first. Only shoddy exegesis can insist that in poetry a second line must be precisely parallel with the first.
   2. It is said that "foundations" cannot be the object of the verb, because there the verb has a disjunctive accent. It should be remembered, however, that the accents were first inserted into the manuscripts by the Masoretes at about A.D. 900. The meaning of many of them is uncertain. If they were all thoroughly understood, we would know only the Jewish exegesis or Jewish tradition of that time. It is hardly conceivable that in every

179

case they represent a tradition going back to the time of original writing. In the opinion of the present writer, insertion here of a preposition that is not contained in the text is unwarranted.

9. The word *servant* naturally occurs in other senses in the earlier part of the book.
10. Hebrew *mishpāt*
11. Hebrew *gōyīm*
12. Hebrew *shālēm*
13. Hebrew *shālam*
14. Another such *pual* participle is in Psalm 18:3 (4), "worthy to be praised."
15. Hebrew *yāsar*
16. Hebrew *gā'al*
17. Greek *sōtēr*
18. Hebrew *mōshī{a}'*
19. Hebrew *bārī{a}ḥ*
20. Verses 19-20 could be interpreted as a reference to God's care for His people during the wilderness journey from Egypt to Canaan.
21. In Isaiah 45:7, the King James rendering "I . . . create evil" can easily give a modern reader the idea that God says that He is the originator of moral evil, since the meaning of the word *evil* has become more limited during the past three centuries. The King James word "evil," like the Hebrew word that it translates (*ra'*), is often used of what is physically destructive or harmful, whether morally good, bad, or indifferent. Modern translations generally render the word in this verse as "calamity," "disaster" or "trouble."
22. Again a prophetic perfect, as in Isaiah 44:22 and 53:8-9.
23. During this long period, Babylon had had its times of great imperial power and its times of humiliation and abasement. Two Assyrian kings claimed to have completely destroyed Babylon; yet in both cases the claim must have been greatly exaggerated, for within a short time the city was again a very important factor. Not long after the second of these alleged destructions, the king of Babylon helped to destroy the Assyrian Empire and established the Neo-Babylonian Empire on its ruins.
24. There is a reference to this practice in Ezekiel 21:21, where the king of Babylon looked at the liver of a slain animal in order to make an important decision.
25. It is the opinion of the author that Isaiah 48 definitely belongs to Part 2 of this section of Isaiah. Yet it is a transition chapter; it contains a few survivals of themes that were common in Part 1 and seldom appear later, but these are generally expressed somewhat differently in chapter 48 than in earlier chapters. Sometimes it is alleged that the whole body of material from chapters 40 to 66 should be considered as made up of three sections (chapters 40-48, 49-57, and 58-66) because the last verse of chapter 48 and the

last verse of chapter 57 are almost identical and are paralleled to some extent by the final verse of chapter 66. Such devices are sometimes used by authors to indicate natural divisions, but should never be taken as in themselves sufficient for this purpose. In this case such a division is clearly wrong for two reasons.

1. There is a marked difference between the material from Isaiah 41 to 56:8 and much of the later material, including the rest of chapter 57.

2. There should not even be a chapter division at the end of chapter 56. The material from 56:9 to 57:21 and that from 58:1 to 59:15 are very similar in nature and are quite different from almost everything between 40:1 and 56:8.

26. "From the time it came to be" is a literal rendering of the Hebrew *mē'ēth h*<sup>e</sup>*yōthāh.* The King James rendering "from the time that it was" can give the same idea. It looks back to the creation.

27. Two terms in verse 4 are sometimes misunderstood. "My judgment" might mean the justice due to the Servant, or the justice that the Servant is to establish. In the light of 42:1-7 the latter is correct. Hebrew *p*<sup>e</sup>*'ullā,* "work," should not be rendered as "recompense" or "reward" (see note above on Isaiah 40:10). The context clearly indicates that the Servant's desires are centered on the accomplishment of the work. There is no suggestion in the passage that His concern is to receive justice or recompense for Himself.

28. Hebrew *lō,* "to him," or *lō',* "not." There is manuscript authority for both.

29. The whole context deals with this worldwide work of the Servant. It is belittling to try to find some minor local meaning for Sinim.

30. Hebrew *bānīm,* "sons"; *bōnīm,* "builders"

31. Hebrew *limmūdīm*

32. The Hebrew imperfect can often be translated as a jussive, as here. It is only occasionally that the jussive form differs from an ordinary imperfect.

33. The Hebrew word used here is *'ōz.*

33*a.* Hebrew *śākal* (*hiphil*)

34. The Hebrew preposition *min* generally means "from." There is a less common use to mean "more than." The common usage fits better here than the less common one adopted by the King James Version at these two points in verse 14.

35. Two fairly ancient translations of the Hebrew altogether missed the nature of the comparison, changing the word "you" in the first part of the verse to "him." However, the Septuagint attests the original "you."

35*a.* Hebrew *shāmēm*

36. The word "sprinkle" represents the Hebrew *nāzā,* which occurs at twenty-three other places in the Old Testament. The Revised Standard Version translates it "sprinkle" in twenty-two of these

## Notes to Particular Points

and "spattered" in one (2 Kings 9:33). Yet in Isaiah 52:15 the Revised Standard Version reads, "so shall he startle many nations," and appends a footnote to "startle": "the meaning of the Hebrew word is uncertain." In view of the many other occurrences of the word, the only basis for such a footnote must be an inability to make sense out of the statement that the Servant "will sprinkle many nations." As we have seen, the apostle Peter found no such difficulty.

The German scholars who originally suggested the meaning "startle" for this verse based the suggestion on the fact that a similar word in Arabic means "to leap." Use of a word in a related language to prove the meaning of a Hebrew word was a common practice of scholars a century ago, but is now generally recognized to be an unsound method. Cognates can suggest possibilities but can never prove them. Since twenty occurrences of the Hebrew verb, including this one, are in the *hiphil* form, which usually conveys a causative idea, these scholars suggested that at this place the Hebrew word should mean "cause to leap," and therefore in this context could mean "cause the nations to leap," and therefore could mean "startle." Since the word is nowhere else used in Hebrew in such a sense, this is a most unlikely supposition, particularly when it is noted that in every one of the four instances where it is used in the *qal* form it refers to the sprinkling or spattering of blood.

The Septuagint renders this clause "many nations shall marvel at him." Most students of the Septuagint feel that at this point its rendering was merely a conjecture.

37. In the two New Testament quotations of this clause (John 12:38; Rom 10:16) only the first of these ideas is involved. There are many quotations in the New Testament where only part of the meaning of an Old Testament statement is involved. Thus in 1 Kings 19:18 God declares that in spite of all the destruction predicted in the preceding verse He will preserve the lives of seven thousand Israelites who have not bowed to Baal. This future prediction necessarily implies that this number of believers has escaped thus far, and it is this part of the thought that is quoted in Romans 11:4. The King James Version mistakenly conformed the Old Testament statement to the New Testament quotation, thus omitting part of the meaning which its form and context require.

38. Hebrew *mak'ōb* and *ḥºlī*
39. Hebrew *nāgūaʻ*
40. Hebrew *mūsār*
41. Hebrew *shālōm*
42. The last two Hebrew words in Isaiah 53:8 are rather elliptical and may be literally translated either "a stroke to whom" or "a stroke to him." If taken as "to whom" this part of the verse will read

182

"for the transgression of my people to whom a stroke (was due)."
If taken as "to him," it will read, "for the transgression of my people a stroke (was) to him." (This latter is the interpretation followed in the King James Version, which reads "was he stricken.")
In the former case it repeats the thought that the suffering was
vicarious; in the latter case it simply reiterates the fact that He
suffered. Since both truths are stated many times elsewhere in this
chapter, it makes little difference which of the two is drawn from
these two words. Either translation fits perfectly with the context.

43. Many recent translations render this conjunction as "though" instead of "because." The conjunction used is identical with the preposition that is ordinarily translated "on." There are many places
in the Old Testament where this preposition used as a conjunction clearly means "because," but there are only two or three cases
where the meaning "though" has been suggested for it, and these
are highly questionable.

44. Hebrew $s^{e\bar{\imath}a}h$

45. Hebrew $n\bar{a}than$

46. Hebrew $w^e$

47. *See* n. 43.

48. Hebrew $h\bar{a}l\bar{a}$

49. Hebrew $'\bar{a}sh\bar{a}m$

50. Hebrew $'\bar{\imath}m$

51. Hebrew $zera'$

52. The infinitive absolute sometimes can be represented by "surely"
(as here in King James Version), but frequently means "continually."

53. Hebrew $m\bar{e}'itt\bar{\imath}$

54. Hebrew $s^edh\bar{a}q\bar{a}$

55. Hebrew $n^em\bar{a}n$

56. Hebrew $hesedh$

57. Hebrew $l^eumm\bar{\imath}m$

# Resources for Study

IT WOULD BE EASY to list dozens of books and articles that deal with the book of Isaiah as a whole or with its latter part. Such books have had only a small part in the preparation of the present volume, which is based on the author's careful study of the Hebrew text over a long period of years. In this study the most useful tools have been Hebrew dictionaries, Hebrew and Greek concordances, and Hebrew grammars. The most important of these are mentioned below.

## DICTIONARIES

Brown, F.; Driver, S. R.; and Briggs, C. A. *A Hebrew and English Lexicon of the Old Testament.* Oxford: Clarendon, 1907.

This is still the most useful dictionary for study of the Old Testament, since it lists every occurrence of all except the most common words, arranging its citations according to variations of meaning and usage. Sometimes its interpretations rest upon guesses, and these are often affected by presuppositions of the writers. Such faults, which are present to at least an equal degree in later dictionaries, are more than compensated by the very full presentation of the evidence from usage. Where the evidence is abundant any dictionary would suffice; where such evidence is scanty, this dictionary makes it possible for the student quickly to become aware of this fact and places at his fingertips references to all pertinent instances. Since modern linguistic study has led to the abandonment of etymology as a source for determination of meaning, and has shown that its value for interpretation is limited to suggesting possibilities, all trained linguists now recognize that only usage can determine the meaning of a word in any particular language. The very full presentation of such evidence makes this by far the most useful dictionary of ancient Hebrew. Its one drawback (and this has been a very substantial one) is the fact that its words are not arranged alphabetically but placed according to assumed three-letter roots, while the page headings list the actual words rather than the roots that must be found in order to locate the words. It is often very difficult to know under what assumed root a word should be placed, and sometimes it becomes necessary to look at as many as three or four different parts of the dictionary before finding the discussion that relates to an uncommon Hebrew word. It is now possible completely to remove this obstacle to use of this dictionary, by the help of Bruce Einspahr, *Index to Brown, Driver and Briggs Hebrew Lexicon* (Chicago: Moody, 1976), which did not appear until the present volume was already in press.

Koehler, L.; and Baumgartner, W. *A Dictionary of the Hebrew Old Testament in English and German.* 1951. 2d. ed. Leiden: E. J. Brill, 1958.

Although it is much more recent, this dictionary is far less useful than the one by Brown, Driver, and Briggs. Evidence from usage is given much less fully, so that it mainly consists in a presentation of the views of its authors, and these are often questionable. It has two great advantages over Brown, Driver, and Briggs, which, it is to be feared, may eventually cause it to supplant the much more useful older dictionary. These advantages are that (1) it arranges words alphabetically instead of under assumed three-letter roots, which makes it far easier to use; and (2) it contains references to more recent articles discussing the meaning of particular words.

In both of these dictionaries the interpretation of unusual words is greatly affected by the critical presuppositions of the authors. The first-mentioned is a far more useful tool for anyone who regards the Bible as the infallible Word of God and desires to determine exactly what it means.

CONCORDANCES

*The Englishman's Hebrew and Chaldee Concordance.* 1843. 5th ed. London: Bagster, 1890.

In this very useful work the Hebrew and Aramaic words are listed alphabetically, and their occurrences are arranged in the order of their appearance in the Old Testament. The words are followed by the King James Version translation of the word, with its immediate context. The citations are intended to be complete, except in the case of extremely common words.

# Resources for Study

Hatch, E.; and Redpath, H. A. *A Concordance to the Septuagint and other Greek Versions of the Old Testament.* 1897. Reprint. Graz, Austria: Akademische Druck, U. Verlagsanstalt, 1954.

Beginning in the second century B.C., the various portions of the Hebrew Old Testament were translated into Greek. Study of the ways various Hebrew words were rendered in Greek at that early time is an invaluable aid for determining the correct meaning of these words and also for seeing how various Old Testament passages were understood at that time. This concordance lists the occurrences of the Greek words in the translations and refers by number to the Hebrew original. The usefulness of this valuable work is greatly increased by Volume 3, which contains a list of the Hebrew and Aramaic words, followed by references to the pages on which translations of it may be found. Unfortunately it does not, as does *Young's Concordance,* state the number of times each word is translated in a particular way. It has occasionally been necessary, in seeking to understand the exact meaning of a Hebrew word used in a difficult passage in Isaiah, to look up as many as fifteen or twenty Greek words in the first two volumes of Hatch and Redpath in order to find out which are frequently used to render the Hebrew word, and to eliminate those that represent rare interpretations or textual erorrs. Despite this disadvantage, this set has been of tremendous aid in the study of this portion of Isaiah.

Lisowsky, G.; and Rost, L. *Koncordanz zum hebräischen Alten Testament, nach dem von Paul Kahle in der Biblia Hebraica edidit R. Kittel besorgten masoretischen Text.* Stuttgart: Württembergische Bibelanstalt, 1958.

Mandelkern, S. *Veteris Testamenti concordantiae Hebraicae atque Chaldaicae.* 1896. 3d ed. Tel-Aviv: Schocken, 1971.

As an aid to determining the exact meaning of a rare word, this is the most useful concordance, since it lists all occurrences, arranged according to the precise forms in which the words are used. If this book is not available, the preceding work is useful.

Strong, J. *Strong's Exhaustive Concordance of the Bible.* 1894. Reprint. Nashville: Abingdon, 1975.

This book is particularly helpful in studying usage of extremely common Hebrew words, since it is more exhaustive than *Young's*. Its arrangement, placing all occurrences of an English word together, regardless of the Hebrew or Greek original, and referring to the original only by a number, makes it generally far less useful for the student.

For many purposes the English-speaking student can find practically all he needs by the use of the following book:

Young, R. *Young's Analytical Concordance to the Bible.* 1879. 22d Am. ed. Reprint. Grand Rapids: Eerdmans, 1975.

This work lists each occurrence of an English word in the King James Version, arranged under the original Hebrew and Greek words. Thus one can tell at a glance whether a word is translated a certain way a great many times in the King James Version or only once or twice. The appendix lists all the Hebrew and Greek words in a rather unscientific arrangement, but one that is easily used even by those who know no Hebrew or Greek. Under each word it lists the various ways it is translated in the King James Version, and the number of times each occurs. If one rendering occurs many times, or if the word is translated by a number of English words with very similar meanings, one can safely conclude that the evidence from usage is quite sufficient to establish a meaning. If, however, a particular rendering occurs only once or twice, the student is justified in examining the passages carefully and forming his own judgment on the basis of usage, which is now recognized to be the only solid basis for such a judgment. Mention in commentaries of related words in Arabic or other cognates may be interesting but should never be regarded as decisive.

### GRAMMARS

Gesenius W. *Hebrew Grammar.* Edited by E. Kautsch. 2d Eng. ed. Revised in accordance with 28th Ger. ed. by A. E. Cowley. Reprint. Oxford: Clarendon, 1910.

This is the only full presentation of classical Hebrew grammar that is available in English. Although written in a cumbersome style and sometimes not very logically arranged, the book refers to most of the important occurrences of Hebrew forms and syntactical usages. As are the dictionaries mentioned above, it is often affected by the presuppositions of its originator and subsequent editors. Yet the fullness of its presentation and the very great number of references make it easy to see where the evidence is so great that one can be fairly safe in accepting a statement as true, and where the evidence is comparatively small, so that one should pursue original investigation. The book contains many conclusions that are not dependable, but it gives the material with which one can study particular problems for himself. Other so-called Hebrew grammars in English are usually introductions to the language, valuable as textbooks but not detailed enough to be of any great value in the study of difficult passages.

## COMMENTARIES

Most commentaries tend to repeat one another's mistakes, and they often jump to conclusions based on the presuppositions of their writers. There is no great profit in playing one off against another. Some commentaries contain useful discussions of linguistic points; others present helpful devotional material. It is rare for one to attempt that comparative study of Scriptural passages that forms a vital part of the approach to this study.

Since most commentaries on Isaiah have been of little help in preparation of this volume, I shall list only three. Although often differing with the conclusions, I have found valuable discussions of particular linguistic points in each of them.

Alexander, J. A. *Commentary on the Prophecies of Isaiah.* 1846. Rev. ed. 1865. Reprint. Grand Rapids: Zondervan, 1971.

Delitzsch, F. *Commentary on Isaiah.* Grand Rapids: Eerdmans, 1973.

There were four editions of this valuable German commentary, published in 1866, 1869, 1879, and 1889. Each of these editions was translated into English. The most easily obtainable translation (from the 2d German edition) is included in the series of Old Testament Commentaries by Keil (C. F.) and Delitzsch, reprinted at Grand Rapids in 1973.

Young, E. J. *The Book of Isaiah.* 3 vols. Grand Rapids: Eerdmans, 1965-72.

# Scripture Index

**189**

# Scripture Index

**190**

# Index of Hebrew Words

The following words, written in transliteration, are arranged, according to their consonants, in the order of the Hebrew alphabet. The standard system of transliteration is used, except that the letter *shīn* is here represented by *sh*. In the case of the letters *b, g, d, k, p, t,* the letter *h* is sometimes added where the soft pronunciation is involved. The system of transliteration can be shown by arranging the transliterated letters in the order of the Hebrew alphabet as follows: ', b, g, d, h, w, z, ḥ, ṭ, y, k, l, m, n, s, ', p, ṣ, q, r, ś, sh, t.